"We're so blessed with golf riches, Tidyman was able to write a great travel book without even crossing a state line. *GP & W* is a celebration of Ohio golf—we have courses from the great designers, hotels that cater to players, and unforgettable restaurants. It's hard to read this book and not make plans!"

—*Dominic Antenucci, Executive Director, Northern Ohio PGA*

"I think lots of golfers will be surprised when they pick up *Golf, Poker and Whiskey*. In Ohio, we have the courses, the lodging, the restaurants to make every getaway memorable. Whose idea was it to have Tidyman scout them and put his reports between the covers of this book? It's a great read!"

—*Jimmy Hanlin, Director of Golf, Little Mountain Country Club*

"I'm keeping one copy of *Golf, Poker and Whiskey* in my golf bag and one copy on the bedside table. As a veteran of many getaways (and often The Guy,) I loved the book. So many golf getaways, so little time."

—*Donald L. Franceski*

Golf, Poker and Whiskey

The Guys' Guide to Ohio Golf Getaways

John H. Tidyman

ORANGE *frazer* PRESS

Wilmington, Ohio

ISBN 978-1933197-760
Copyright©2010 John H. Tidyman

Additional copies of *Golf, Poker and Whiskey: The Guys' Guide to Ohio Golf Getaways* may be ordered directly from:
Orange Frazer Press
P.O. Box 214
Wilmington, OH 45177

Telephone 1.800.852.9332 for price and shipping information.
Website: *www.orangefrazer.com*

Book and cover design: Chad DeBoard, Orange Frazer Press

Library of Congress Control Number: 2010934440

For Annabelle Lee Dowd, keeper of my heart.

TABLE *of* CONTENTS

SOUTHEAST

SOUTHWEST

ACKNOWLEDGEMENTS

You quickly learn how big Ohio is when you write about its golf riches. Here are the men and women who traversed the state, fearlessly teeing it up at unfamiliar courses, resting their heads on pillows not their own, ordering without care strip steaks and mashed potatoes, shouting, "ante up," proudly ignorant of local gambling laws, and striking up conversations with head golf professionals, maître d's, hoteliers and waitresses of all sort. From this perilous journey, all safely returned home, pockets stuffed with notes, interview tapes, dog-eared scorecards, and a greater appreciation for this golfer's heaven, Ohio.

Without their valorous service, this volume would have been a multi-year project. Allow me to toast and salute: Anton Don, Paul Murphy, George Jacynycz, Terence Uhl, Barbara Uhl, Ann Stasko, Paul Roetzer, Billy Leitch, Fran Carey, Barry Goodrich, George Hrbek, and Bob Gainer. Among the group is a barber, a CPA, a landscaper, a Lutheran minister, a sportswriter, a hotel executive, a radio producer, a hospital technician, a trio of salesmen, and a communications executive.

When golf called, each stood and delivered.

— John H. Tidyman

INTRODUCTION

Know why we're addicted to golf? Hope. Every time we address the ball, regardless of recent history, we believe we're going to perfectly hit it. It's like the feeling we enjoy walking out of the confessional, learning the seized engine is covered by warranty, winning Pick 4, or listening to our parole officer say, "Well, that's it. I hope I never see you again."

With golf, unlike those other examples, the wondrous feeling of hope is there, maybe 80, 90, or 110 times per round.

Here's another reason. We can duplicate many of the shots made by the touring professionals. Unlike the guys in other sports, we'll never throw a 90-mph brushback, recover an onside kick, hire an agent, or be banned from the sport for drugs or gambling.

But with Tour players, we have some fellow travelers. We have chipped in from sidehill lies, blasted out of sand and watched the ball drop, firmed in a five-foot putt. The big hitters among us hit drives that sail more than 300 yards.

But we don't do it consistently, shot after shot after shot. That's obvious: The vast majority of trunk slammers never break 90.

On the touring pro's side, there are guys who jiggle when they waggle, four-putt greens, drink and smoke too much, say bad words, and make clubs act like helicopter rotors.

They are us. We are them.

It is that physical and emotional connection that allows us to enjoy watching golf, either in person, or on the television. More than that, it helps us enjoy playing.

There is nothing new about golf getaways. They are big business and big fun. With the economy still shaky and Congress still trying to understand derivatives, getaways to the Carolinas, Florida, and the Upper Peninsula will be out of reach for many.

That's the bad news.

The good news is the incredible wealth of getaways in Ohio. Whether a luxurious resort or a cabin in the woods, we have them in abundance. Want to play a course created by a particular designer? Who? We have Mike Hurdzan and Dana Fry, Donald Ross, Arthur Hills, Tom Fazio, Brian Huntley, Barry Serafin, Tom Weiskopf and many others. New course, old course, championship course, renovated course, historic course? All here.

Where would you like to stay? A boutique hotel? A resort on the edge of Lake Erie? A cabin in the woods? A first-class hotel? A bed and breakfast so sweet you want to stay? Got it, got it, got it, got it, and got it.

Hungry? How about frog legs or raw oysters? Lake Erie perch and walleye? A perfectly grilled flat iron steak or a belt-loosening porterhouse? Pasta and sauces as you've never before enjoyed? A bottle or two of Ohio wines that have a national reputation? Shots and beers served here, along with Rob Roys, Sidecars, Manhattans, aperitif d'absinthe. Your table is this way, sir.

This book doesn't cover the waterfront. The subject is big enough for a sackful of books. But this book should be encouragement for you to call and say, "Hi, I want to book a getaway for twelve guys."

If you come across hidden gems, or want to heap praise (or dung) on a trip, by all means, let me know. Until then, see you at the turn.

John H. Tidyman
forgedirons@yahoo.com

THE GUY

Can we praise The Guy too much? Heck, no. The Guy who puts these getaways together for us is to golf getaways what the lead dog is to Iditarod: We'd be lost without him. His roles and responsibilities, which settle comfortably on his broad shoulders, are many and vital to the success of a getaway.

He doesn't seek the position as much as the position seeks him. The Guy is a natural. For the rest of us, the getaway begins when we toss the sticks in the trunk, double-check our wardrobe, make sure the wallet has lots of cash in it, and set off.

Not so for The Guy. The getaway, for him, begins when he decides which courses and which hotels will be blessed with our business. Just as the rest of us are buoyed with anticipation when we back out of the driveway, so is The Guy, when he makes that first phone call to the hotel and announces, "Hello, I'd like to arrange a golf getaway for my group."

But long before that first phone call, he has been in touch with each of us, asking questions and jotting down the answers: Can you go on such-and-such a date? These are the preliminary costs; can you send me a deposit by such-and-such a date? Write this down: If you have to cancel, I have to know by such-and-such a date. What's your current handicap? Anybody you absolutely don't want to play with? Share a room with?

He thinks about his players. No sense having a 32-handicap play with an 11-handicap. Try not to put a slow poke, one who reads every green before three putting, with someone who plays at a brisk pace. Arrange the slower players to tee it up at the end of the line. (We had a new player once. Who knew that he constantly whistled? Lucky he wasn't found floating in a water hazard.)

Arrange any games, such as best-ball, blind bogie, (we know one Guy who always adds a day of match play), or alternate shot.

Guys on getaways are not, by and large, big on prizes. Except the money from golf bets and cards, of course. But we once had a Guy who believed the best player should go home with a trophy. So he'd drop by a thrift shop and pick up a trophy for a buck or so. That the winner was awarded a trophy with a bowler on top, inscribed, "Most Improved Bowler, 1966, Mahall's Twenty Lanes," meant nothing. What meant something was the trophy itself and today, those trophies sit on mantles reserved for portraits of the in-laws. To say those trophies serve as great conversation pieces is almost redundant.

The Guy does two more things: First, he double-checks on everything. If one of us doesn't show up for breakfast, he makes sure he is re-awakened. No sense showing up at the hotel and listening to the manager say, "Oh, there are sixteen of you? Hmm, I thought it was six." Or showing up at the course and having the starter say, "Oh, you're down for four foursomes, but it's for tomorrow. We got league play out there right now." Second, he's the go-to guy if problems arise, the buffer between hotel management or the pro at the course. About the only thing he doesn't take care of is weather, though some Guys have been known to offer up a Novena or two for sun and low humidity.

Through it all, he thinks about his own game and tries to enjoy the getaway. When the troops come home, some call with complaints or recommendations. Both go into his futures file.

How to thank The Guy? Remember, he is thanked for his service and, at the same time, bribed to do it next time, so the gift should be thoughtful. Bottle of good whiskey should do it.

Golf, Poker and Whiskey

MAUMEE BAY
STATE PARK

1400 State Park Rd.
Oregon
419.836.7758
www.maumeebaystateparklodge.com

If we set you up to play a round with Arthur Hills at his wonderful course at **Maumee Bay State Park**, would you take us to lunch?

A couple times every season, Hills arrives at his course and enjoys eighteen holes. Here's how you get to play with him: be the luckiest golfer in the state. That will mean arriving on the same day Hills arrives, and then nonchalantly saying something like, "Need a fourth, Arthur?" If he says yes, your place in golf history is pretty much assured.

Hills, of Toledo, plays the course a time or two every season. One time he arrived in the middle of a drought. Fairways were no harder than the asphalt in the parking lot, but no less, either. Green speeds were not measured by Stimpmeters, but by radar guns.

He said that these were the conditions for which he designed the course. That, in our opinion, was Hills paying homage to good golfers, the guys who really do think before every shot. More than that, they're planning for the next shot at the same. Those players take into account course conditions with the same intimacy Indianapolis 500 drivers study track conditions. Mortals such as us are limited to the easy ones, such as, 'Are we getting lots of roll?' and, 'What time do you think the frost will burn off?'

The single-digit handicappers want to know the precise speed of the greens, which way and how hard is the wind blowing, the effect of grain on the green, the texture of the sand, and just how much risk they can eliminate from a risk-and-reward shot. They can compare and contrast the virtues of bump-and-run and pitching.

These are the guys who understand a television announcer saying, "The only bailout is to the left of the green." Man, we have no idea what a bailout is. We mean besides spending tax dollars to keep Wall Street criminals living well on the Upper West Side.

This state park resort is pretty new, built in 1991, on 1,850 acres, and the style reflects that. Instead of timbers throughout, the place is stone and glass, comfort and elegance. The drinking, dining and golf are good examples. Only 120 rooms, and tucked in the northwest corner of the state.

The terrain here, hard by Lake Erie, is flat, which added to Hills's design challenge. Our educated guess is that he thrives on design challenges. His success is evident from every tee box, but we played the whites, only 6,136 yards, and came away purely amazed. Who knew his fairways, with insidious undulations (undulations, after all, is a word usually reserved for putting greens,) would confound us for a while, then convert us?

And just how, on this featureless track, did he hide those pot bunkers, not to be discovered until we were forced to climb in and out? What's this business about fescue? We thought when we started we would lose no more than two balls. That's what it looked like. Funny thing about fescue: If you hit into it, you'll find a ball. Won't be your ball, but it will be a ball. We should add that fescue is a design tool that should be used more widely. It not only provides shape and direction to a hole, but the stuff is gorgeous. From a maintenance viewpoint, how much care and feeding can it need?

Maybe we were seduced by the opening hole, a pleasant par 4 of only 373 yards. The unrealistic member of our group has a habit of yelling, as he approaches a short approach, "I smell birdie." That optimism didn't last long. We're ardent fans of short par 4s, and No.

2, just a little over 300 yards, has rules from tee to green. First, unless you have the 155 mm howitzer in the bag, forget about it, okay? Fools rush in where brave men fear to tread. But with an accurate tee shot, life starts looking pretty good. For an inaccurate tee shot, bogey starts looking pretty good. Plenty of sand, and if your shot nestles in the tall grasses, we warned you. It's not a hard hole, but one that demands some restraint.

Water comes into play on the next few holes, notably the lake that hugs the entire right side of No. 3 and plays a starring role (by hugging and refusing to let go) on No. 5, too, the first par 5. The home hole on the front side is also the number one handicap hole and with the water down the left side, you finally get a chance to play your slice (or, as you call it, your power fade) as if it were intentional. Take care, though, and check the wind before flailing away.

There is only one reason to stop at the turn, and that is to see if Mr. Hills is there and looking for a fourth. Other than that, grab an energy drink, check that your scapular is facing out, and back at it.

No. 10 is just like No. 9, except it goes in the opposite direction. Equally challenging, equally beautiful. If you liked *Lost*, you'll love No. 14, which has everything except the fat guy who somehow never loses weight. The home hole is a short par 5, but between fairway and green is substantial water.

This being a resort course, the maintenance is darn near perfect. There's a good pro shop and staff members love to brag about their course and its designer.

We get a choice for lodging, and while cottages are available (big, private, well-equipped, and home to some of the greatest card games in golf getaway history), we stayed at the lodge because, well, it's a resort lodge. Every room has a balcony. Not much of a balcony, but think of it: fresh coffee, first cigaret and a view of Lake Erie. It is inspiring.

(We tightly closed the balcony doors lest we be found enjoying the noxious weed. At many places, evidence of smoking is punishable by a substantial charge.)

And the best part: The sliding front door is a mere 300 yards from the clubhouse.

(Inside skinny: Getaway or no getaway, with the rates charged here, a day trip is always a good idea. Or as one of us astutely noted, "They're givin' it away.")

Getaways are more than golf, of course, and here we enjoyed dinner, lodging, and nuclear power. What could be more reassuring than enjoying a thick steak and cold beer while gazing through the tall windows at the Davis Besse nuclear plant? No other structure has quite the lines or shape that a cooling tower provides.

The restaurant is Deck of Water's Edge, and offers a menu of comfort food as well as the stuff you see created on television. We were handed over to a waitress who was more than professional; she was eager to know where we came from and whether we had been there before and were we enjoying ourselves. Between her and scandalously low green fees, one of us announced, "I don't need a getaway package. All I gotta do is get up at 5:30 and I can spend a day here."

Maumee Bay State Park

(1) Par 4

32
81
124
176
195

423
394
373
340

(2) Par 4

24
79
100
126
150

347
331
317
287

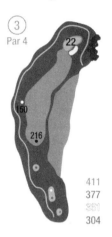

(3) Par 4

22
150
216

411
377
351
304

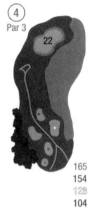

(4) Par 3

22

165
154
128
104

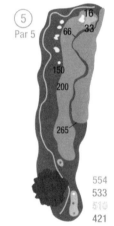

(5) Par 5

16
66 33
150
200
265

554
533
510
421

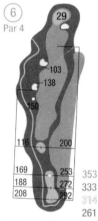

(6) Par 4

29
103
138
150

116   200

169   253   353
188   272   333
208   292   314
              261

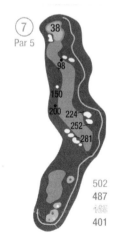

(7) Par 5

38
98
150
200 224
252
281

502
487
466
401

(8) Par 3

34

188
170
145
120

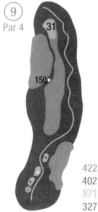

(9) Par 4

31
150

422
402
371
327

Maumee Bay State Park

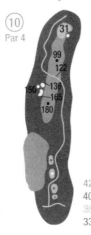

(10) Par 4

31
99
122
150 136
165
180

423
404
366
334

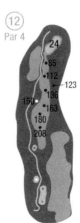

(11) Par 3

35

187
168
150
113

(12) Par 4

24
85
112 123
136
150 163
180
208

450
426
332
302

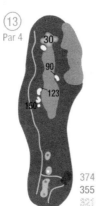

(13) Par 4

30
90
123
150

374
355
321
289

(14) Par 5

27
94
150
195
200

525
511
461
409

(15) Par 3

32

222
197
179
143

(16) Par 4

38
101
133
150 174
219

453
412
384
315

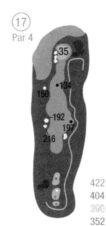

(17) Par 4

35
134
150
192
197
216

422
404
380
352

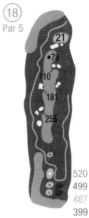

(18) Par 5

21
73
10
181
255

520
499
467
399

SAWMILL CREEK RESORT

400 Sawmill Creek Dr. W

Huron

800.729.6455

www.sawmillcreek.com

LEMMY'S RESTAURANT

2027 Cleveland Rd. W

Huron

419.433.5501

Ah, **Sawmill Creek Resort**. It's almost a little town. Once you pull in, you want for nothing, and the car sits until you're ready to leave. Sawmill sits on the shores of western Lake Erie, offers more comforts than we deserve, and boasts a Tom Fazio course.

True story. A few years ago, we called Fazio, in Hendersonville, N.C., for an interview. Talk about your down home kind of guy. He answered the phone. He was thoughtful, gracious, and unhurried. We suggested, at one point, that his office walls were filled with pictures from his great courses: Karsten Creek, Pinehurst No. 4, The Quarry at La Quinta, his renovation work at Augusta National.

We suggested wrong.

The walls were filled with pictures of his family. Six kids and a wife. Fazio is the designer who turned down jobs overseas because he didn't want to be separated from his family. His work schedule in America was heavily influenced by the wife and kids: He didn't want to miss Little League games, or Christmas, or graduation ceremonies. He didn't.

In northern Ohio, he built two terrific courses; Sand Ridge, a private club in Chardon, and Sawmill Creek. This one can play up to 6,700 yards, but remember, par is only 71. The lakeside terrain is flat, and the winds whistling across off Lake Erie can come into play. Lots of northern Ohio players make a stop or two here every season. We know many players go ga-ga over autumn colors on courses and this place will do, but our favorite time here is the middle of summer, maybe early August, when the air couldn't be stirred with a spoon, when even the weeping willows droop more than usual, and players wearing designer double knit pants dream of the khaki shorts they left in the room. That time of year, Sawmill is lush; it's when the contrast is most distinct between blue lake, green course, bright sand and trees as full as they're going to get.

Playing a flat resort course sounds like an opportunity to score our personal best. That may be, but not without playing Sawmill a half dozen or so times. No one would call it a subtle course, but the subtleties sit between you and your best round. Sort of like God is in the details.

Not to sound like know-it-alls, but in our experienced opinion, a ball landing in the creek belongs in the creek. Those are new golf shoes, not new hiking boots.

The first hole is a straightway par 4 with a very accessible green, if the pin isn't behind the front right hazard, which makes it a sucker pin. Good warm up, we agreed, but the double bogey guy with us landed his drive in the rough. He thought it was deeper than it looked and wondered if the rough might be sneaky penal.

No. 2 is a reminder of Sawmill's good looks. Behind the faraway green, we see only mature trees and beyond that nothing but blue sky. The next hole is the first par 5, and it's short. It's also a dogleg with sand, water and marsh reminding us to keep it in the short grass. Got a big gun in the bag? Leave it there.

Okay, we know this violates the Rules of Golf, but we love to play par 5s and par 3s from the tips, regardless where our normal tee box is. No. 5 is a good example why we do it. It's par 3, 128 yards from the whites, but an extra thirty yards from the tips. It's scary-looking, with sand protecting the right left, and a creek sashaying into play on the right. The falloff from the right side of fairway into the creek is steep. It's probably better to leave the ball there than retrieve it, only because golfers retrieving balls from such hazards are a regular staple on *America's Funniest Home Videos.*

We played No. 7 the same way. The par 3 is 170 from the whites, but 188 from the blues. Like his last par 3, Fazio scared us when we arrived at the tee. As if it were not enough to protect his green with sand and water, he jacked up the green, too, and failing to add at least one club can be disastrous. Not to sound like know-it-alls, but in our experienced opinion, a ball landing in the creek belongs in the creek. Those are new golf shoes, not new hiking boots.

At No. 9, we walked to the tips just to see what the very good players see. Whew. All we saw was water. It doesn't start until the approach, but water jams its way into the left side of this hole like your first wife used to finish your sentences, which is to say, a major distraction. The second line of defense is sand. From the blues, 409 yards; from the whites, 357 yards. Doesn't make any difference: If you're on in regulation, likely you brought your A game.

Playing this hole in par is satisfying and a great way to head over to Mulligan's Pub, where our drink orders said something about us: one gin and tonic, two Cokes, and one beer with pretzels. (He says the oil from potato chips, which he prefers, leaves cooking oil on his fingertips and interferes with his grip.)

We had to wait a little bit at the turn, and the topic of conversation was the scorecard. How could we be shooting higher than our handicaps on a flat course with little wind? We agreed Sawmill calls for a confident short game, one in which putting some backspin on a chip is a definite virtue, and skill in judging breaks and speed on the green.

Boy, did we screw up on No. 12, a par 5 that should have played

554 yards for us, but in our ignorance, we stepped back and played 568 yards. Even from the whites, this hole is dangerous. Unpredictable. Probably irrigated with one half water and one half blood. You know when a single-digit handicapper starts trembling at the tee, something's amiss. Next time we play, we'll all get gin and tonics at the turn.

Water comes into play on both sides, the usual suspects—sand hazards and trees—almost announce, "We were here first," and one of the green's virtues it took from pinball: tilt.

The home hole is benign compared to some others, but the outcome of the match shouldn't depend on it.

So after this, what are you, hungry or tired? That's what we like about having the restaurant and bar within stumbling distance to the room.

Sawmill went up a long time ago, 1972, and could use some renovation, but by and large, it's comfortable. Especially the room reserved for The Guy. Fireplace and jacuzzi. It's not easy concentrating on a poker hand when the bath is creating a bathtub massage, and you're not in it. So it goes.

Dinner was at one of the three restaurants here, Salmon Run. Little inside skinny for you: The house garden salad here is one of the best house salads ever. Period.

Our restaurant reviewing skills are lacking and it shows in what we ordered: One order of Lake Erie perch and three strip steaks. We passed on the Pacific halibut, mostly because the Pacific is so far from here. Also, none of us could explain the vanilla bean buerre blanc sauce with crispy capers. Part of the salmon dinner included rubbing the poor fish with ginger and green curry sauce.

We're not dessert aficionados, but in the interest of completeness, we watched a waiter bring to a good-looking blonde a fudge lava cake a la mode. When we were leaving, the bravest of the group walked over, nodded to her date, and asked her if she enjoyed it. Her answer was a really big smile and a soft growl, so we figure it was very good.

When we left Sawmill for home, we found a great little neighborhood place for lunch. It is called **Lemmy's Restaurant,** and don't ask us why. It's not big, we assumed it to be owner-operated, and we loved it. Breakfast all day and perch so fresh we suspect Lemmy's nephews and nieces are out back, putting shiners on double rigs and hauling them in.

Ah, for the life of a club pro. Stand around in the pro shop, listening to the trials and tribulations of players. Answering questions with the solemnity and assuredness of a minor god. Lunch in the clubhouse, sometimes a few blessed players invited to the table. Looking good with a $90 shirt, $120 pair of golf knit slacks, and who knows what he paid for those shoes? In the afternoon, a round of golf followed by one or two beers. Then into the luxury car for home.

If that were only so. You think you want the job. You don't.

As well dressed, knowledgeable, and talented as a PGA professional is, he works harder than a barber in boot camp. Think relentless. It is non-stop from the time they arrive, which is before sunrise, until they turn out the lights and lock the door, which is after the sun sets.

The work load and schedule didn't begin when he was named head golf professional. From his first job, maybe cart manager or bag boy, the long hours have been part and parcel of the career.

Getting from apprenticeship to head golf professional is a long and arduous career path, and not everyone makes it. The PGA insists on a great deal of education, testing, and service to the game. Any club pro with PGA behind his name, and a professional designation of 1-A, has dedicated his life to the game. No two ways about it.

The term multi-tasking was created to describe these guys. They know they're going to spend a career in a sandwich: on one side is the owner or president of the course and on the other is the customer. Both are vital.

Not saying every club pro has this schedule, but in one form or another, they jam all these chores into a single day:

1. Open the place, make sure all the staff is aboard, hand out orders that might include, wash the pro shop windows, call the trash hauler and see why the dumpster didn't get emptied yesterday, refill the soapy water in the ball washers, move the tees on the practice range, inventory the pro shop, review the tee times for the day, make sure carts are gassed up and clean.

2. Make time to listen to salesmen who think their new ball, shoe, shirt, umbrella, advertising vehicle, phone system, tee, grass seed, security system, yardage markers, sun visor, or GPS system will make the pro's life easier and his customers happier.

3. His partner is the course superintendent. They will talk about the schedule for fertigation or irrigation, the condition of the greens and bunkers, plans for aerating the greens, the snow fungus that showed up on the back of the seventeenth green, any problems with the mowing equipment, and raises for the superintendent's staff.

4. Along the way, the club pro will handle any number of telephone calls and work with callers setting up outings. He has to prepare a budget for the caller, based on number of players, details for the dinner, scoring assistance, how the course should be set up, and plans for bad weather.

5. He has to get over to the driving range where a student waits for a lesson. The PGA places high value on teaching. How else are we going to get the next generation hooked on Proof That God Loves Us? The pro concentrates on the student's swing, noticing the little things that have big effect on ball flight. More than one student a day is common.

He knows he represents the club and course, that the way he treats his staff and customers goes a long way towards a profitable operation. Think about it. Ever see a club pro lose his temper?

In Ohio, there are two PGA sections, north and south. Eleven hundred men and women belong and the PGA does more than we could ever imagine for us and the game of golf.

While many club professionals have a faith, maybe Jewish, Muslim, Catholic, Pagan, Protestant, those faiths are secondary. Every good golf pro is, at heart, Buddhist. Buddha said, "One thing I teach: suffering and the end of suffering." If that isn't golf, what is?

The pro is off on Mondays, a good day to sleep in, see the dentist, post bond for his son, get the emissions test and new plates for the car, play a round of golf, remind his wife who he is, fill out his absentee ballot, and do his weekly rendition of yelling at the dog, which always begins (and ends) with, "If you're living under my roof, you're going to obey my rules."

Many golf pros say in their next life, they'd like to be the Border collie at the course. Lay around, get petted and fed, chase a bunch of geese. That would be plenty.

THUNDERBIRD HILLS GOLF CLUB

1316 Mudbrook Rd.

Huron

419.433.4552

www.thunderbirdhills.com

THE ANGRY BULL

3317 Cleveland Rd. E

Huron

419.433.2933

KALAHARI WATER RESORT PARK

7000 Kalahari Dr.

Sandusky

877.525.2427

The Angry Bull has our kind of bar: L-shaped. It makes conversation easier and when we're not conversing, makes listening unavoidable. The bar is not big, and the TV hanging in the corner is, by today's standards, small. Just the way we like it.

No wimps among us. Two Manhattans, two Rob Roys. Now that's the way to enjoy a generous cocktail before dinner. We showed up, freshly shaved and showered, a little early. If there's one thing we love about walking into a steakhouse, it's the aroma. Between watching the wait staff balance plates of hot beef, and that wonderful smell, anticipation grows and mouths water. Both booths and tables in the dining room; we took over a six-top for the four of us and used all of the space.

Waitresses like us. We're low maintenance. Stiff drink, thick steak, and good potatoes. What else does a man need? Plus, the more we drink, the higher we tip. It's a man thing.

We had a couple plates of appetizers only because we never saw walleye served as an appetizer. Strips of fillet, lightly breaded, nicely fried. Perfect.

Big steaks served here. The porterhouse is a pound and a half, the ribeye is a full pound, and—get this—the large serving of prime rib is two pounds.

It reminded us of one of our late, great, playing partners, who loved his beef so rare, he would tell the waitress, "Just gimme a knife and push the cow past me."

The prime rib can be sliced a little thinner, too, so plates of one pound or three quarters of a pound can be enjoyed. And all four of us had mashed potatoes. Dinner was a meal for men on a golf getaway.

Oh, yeah, the golf. **Thunderbird Hills Golf Club**, like Firestone, has a North and South course. Thunderbird is way more fun. The demarcation line between courses is a wide one, State Route 6, and getting from one to the other means a short drive over the bridge. If ever a club was built for thirty-six holes a day, this is it. Both courses share some virtues and both are markedly different from each other.

Among the virtues, playability, maintenance, great staff, and accessibility. But two different courses they are. The North is hillier and has lots more trees. The South is essentially flat and wide open.

As if we needed more reasons not to load up at the turn with hot dogs, tater chips, and beer.

And No. 1 on the North is an opening hole we'll never forget. It's a par 5, and paying homage to the Eisenhower Tree at Augusta, features a noble oak tree in the middle of the fairway. It can get in the way of the approach, but what we did was just aim right at it. No one hit it and we found ourselves out of harm's way for the next shot.

The blues and the whites play the same tee on No. 2, a short par 3 of 130 yards. As the eighteenth handicap hole, its resistance to par is like Tiger's resistance to babes. Still, over-hitting means sleeping with the fishes. Not that it happened to us, but what if, on the opening hole, your second shot tangled with an oak leaf cluster and you ended up taking a seven. And then, on No. 2, you pick the wrong club and end up in the water behind the green. Geez—a dozen strokes after only playing two holes?

The challenge doesn't let up at the next tee, a short par 4 with a split fairway and water in front of the green. Sheesh!

We're making it sound more difficult than it is. The North course is very pretty and play here is quick. Of course you can get into trouble; getting out is a simple matter, though it often precludes the possibility of par.

The front side finishes with the second par 5, this one 535 yards, and by this time, we're used to the ebb and flow of the terrain. The hole bends a bit to the right, but getting on in two is chancy because the second shot is from an uphill lie. Or a downhill lie. Or a sidehill lie. Or any combination thereof.

As if we needed more reasons not to load up at the turn with hot dogs, tater chips, and beer: No. 10, which we considered the North course signature hole. Four hundred forty-five yards, with water sliding across the middle. And the green is elevated. No pars in our group. No. 11 is another short par 3, only 120 yards. Yeah, it's only 120 yards, but there's slope enough in this green that three-putts and worse are common. Gorgeous home hole, all 400 yards of it, and the fairway was treated by tectonic plates before being turned into a fairway. Par here is four and if you score par, then your next move is probably collecting bets in the clubhouse.

From the whites, it's not a long course, 6,347 yards, par 72. But it calls for such a wide variety of shots that the impatient will miss out on pars they could have had. The North course starts by insisting players think and ends the same way. All in all, this is one of the most fun courses we played.

Just south is the, uh, South course, and while they are brother courses, they appear to be sired by different fathers. The South is as flat as the North is rolling. The South is open while North uses more trees to keep us on the right path.

We know they're brothers because the opening hole, a par 5 of 475 yards, also has an oak tree in the middle of the fairway. Not yet a mighty oak, but a couple of generations hence, it will be as intimidating as its brother across the way. At this point, it gets only momentary attention.

The first par 3 is unlike the other course, too: No. 3 is 170 yards from the whites, with big water waiting for slices. Even a straight tee shot has to overcome a couple of ambushes: big sand at the green and a putting surface given to trickery. Find your line and accelerate through.

The first par 5 is No. 5, and while it appears short on the scorecard at a mere 460 yards, those yards are not in a straight line. Not only does the dogleg go left, there are trees aplenty. For the shorter, straighter hitters among us, this is a great birdie opportunity.

No. 9 suddenly bares teeth we didn't know it had: Only 360 yards, the landing area is tighter than Aunt Louise's corset. Miss it and you're swimming, pal. If the drive lands in the short stuff, give pause before selecting an iron because it's an uphill shot to the green. The wind off Lake Erie is often an additional factor.

It doesn't stop at No. 10, another par 5. This one is 510 yards. The fun is that the tee shot is downhill. The concerns are two, a pond that accepts slices and a narrow landing area.

Okay, let's just say that on No. 15, you hit it so sweet the ball develops diabetes. One hundred fifty-five yards from the whites and an elevated tee. And let's say for once the Great Goddess of Golf grants you stop-action. There you are, high finish, hips perfectly turned, the ball almost at the apex of its flight, and that big, flowing Huron River behind the green.

Were you ever part of a more beautiful picture? No, you weren't.

Man, they love their finishing holes here, don't they? The home hole is also the number one handicap, and with good reason. A blind tee shot, canted fairway, couple varieties of water: creek and pond. As we said, these courses are more fun than a fat kid sitting on a birthday cake.

If you take the Thunderbird golf package assembled by **Kalahari Water Resort Park**, there are benefits not available on other getaways. First, before you leave home, you can assemble the little monsters along with She Who Must Be Obeyed and explain, with appropriate seriousness, that you are going to *scout* Kalahari, with an eye towards taking the assemblage at some later date. Second, you can toss inhibition to the wind and have a riot going down the water slides. Third, unless you regularly have coffee on Times Square, at no other getaway was the people-watching better.

Kalahari is comfortable in ways different than most lodging we enjoyed on this tour. We mean, when was the last time you swam up to a bar? Even as we're writing this, we're smiling. If you don't think that was fun, we're going to check your pulse. Kalahari is a little on the loud side, of course, and we found ourselves adding to the chorus.

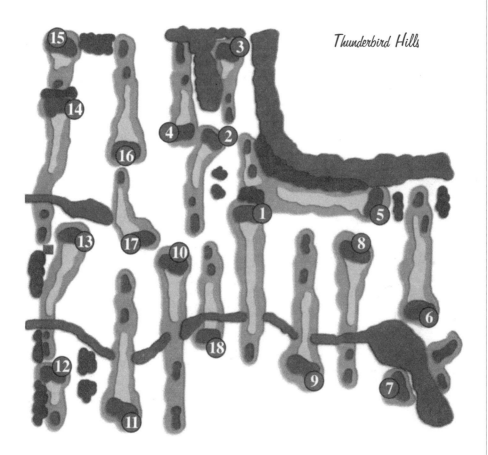

Thunderbird Hills

EAGLE CREEK GOLF CLUB
2406 New State Rd.
Norwalk
419.668.8535
www.eaglecreekgolf.com

GEORGIAN MANOR INN
123 West Main St.
Norwalk
800.668.1644

BLUTO'S SPORTS BAR AND GRILL
33 East Seminary St.
Norwalk
419.668.8862

There are any number of hotels in the area, but we went to the **Georgian Manor Inn** to avoid the screaming hordes going to nearby Cedar Point. Good thinking. The Inn is so elegant, so handsome, so comfortable, that our level of profanity dropped to zero. Even poker seemed roughshod. Instead of money on the table, we should have had some antique poker chips. Instead of excusing ourselves to go out for a cigaret, we should have taken a bejeweled snuff box from our vests and sprinkled snuff on our clenched fists.

Just as we often dress for dinner, here we dressed for poker. It is one of the stops on this statewide tour where forgetting a camera is a major disappointment. Think of it. You, in smoking jacket and ascot, hair slicked back, enjoying a volume on the history of First Ladies. One of us put on airs and called for the butler. "James, a glass of sherry, please." He was not answered.

And the Inn, while not built for card players, offers card rooms second to none. The library was our favorite, though the living room was a close second. Speaking of rating amenities, we couldn't agree which was better, going to bed or waking up. The Manor's idea of reveille is played by birds and water splashing into the pond. Frogs provide the bass line.

There are four magnificent rooms here, each named: Lady Katherine, Lady Anne, Lord Sheldon, and the Georgian. The last time we saw furnishings like this, it was on PBS.

And breakfast. Nine a.m., sir, and you enjoy fresh strawberry French toast. Tomorrow morning, plan on a tender mushroom and onion quiche. Little wonder the Inn has a four-diamond rating from AAA. Here's how special that designation is: There are only a dozen other four-diamond hotels in the entire state. The owners have offered golf packages for a while.

Speaking of things that sparkle, **Eagle Creek Golf Club** has four and a half stars from *Golf Digest*. Brian Huntley was given the job of designing Eagle Creek, and it opened just a dozen or so years ago. The protégé of Arthur Hills created a course that looks so natural, we wondered how much work he really had to do, which is high praise.

Now, we wouldn't use this word when describing a course, but a regular we talked with in the clubhouse said the layout was "lyrical," to which we asked, "Say what?" He explained how the course fit the terrain, how it glides, how it resembles a sensuous dance. How are you going to argue with a guy like that?

Want to walk or ride? Eagle Creek is eminently walkable and there are no time restrictions for setting off on foot. Couple of us walked and carried and loved it. It's by walking we see the big picture as well as the details. The first hole is just what we like best: a straightaway par 5 with minimal obstacles to par. As is our custom, we played the par 5s and par 3s from the tips. From the waybacks, it is 6,603 yards, par 71. Except for our custom, though, we played the whites, which are a wedge over 6,000 yards.

On No. 1, our custom stretches it to 502 yards, and no reason why getting on in regulation can't provide a birdie opportunity. Except.

(There's always an except, isn't there?) The big, lush greens. Getting on in regulation doesn't mean getting close. While we know that the size of the greens has to complement the entire hole, we also think that big greens, with their additional maintenance expense, are also an indication of the course quality. That is, if a big green is perfectly manicured, the course is likely a very good one. Plus, it's such a riot watching a 45-footer curl softly and on its last turn, rattle the bottom of the cup. More luck than skill, maybe, but still...

That guy in the clubhouse, the one who thought the course was lyrical, may have been more accurate than we thought. The bent grass fairways are cut to be shapely instead of straight, and the definition adds to the visual pleasure. It is as if the landing area, either corset-tight or beer-belly wide, was the result of daily decisions by the mower. Especially wide frog hairs here, by the way.

He explained how the course fit the terrain, how it glides, how it resembles a sensuous dance.

Huntley needed only about three dozen sand bunkers to make holes resistant to par, and many of them are around the greens. With water playing a role in eleven holes, there is resistance enough. No. 4 has all the water it needs. A short par 4 of 330 yards, worm burners drown.

There are five par 3s on this course, and most players agree No. 8 is the best. At 159 yards from the tips, you can't miss short without drowning a ball and you can't miss to either side of this narrow green without making par a little more challenging.

At Canterbury CC, in suburban Cleveland, the rolling course has been home to lots of championships of the major sort: thirteen of them, including the PGA Championship, the U.S. Open, the U.S. Senior Open, you get the idea. The finishing three holes there can make or break a score, the toughest trio since Tinkers to Evans to Chance. A par 5, par 3, and par 4, in that order.

Same thing at Eagle Creek, though it's par 3, par 4, and a par 5. If ever you needed an energy bar, with a Gatorade on the side, the tee box at No. 16 is it. No. 18 is long, at 525 yards, because the fairway is narrow. Trees, water and sand wait in ambush between you and the putting surface. Nothing particularly bad about a bogey here, but a par is cause for a fist pump.

A good place to review the game and the course is **Bluto's Sports Bar and Grill**, where a sumptuous repast of cold beer and hot wings almost guarantees really crazy dreams.

For a real supper, the sort your mom would serve you and your hoodlum friends, it's Berry's, and you can bet most of the customers there are locals. If you can clean your plates, from soup to nuts (or coconut cream pie), loosening your belt by two notches is normal. And, yes, the service is always this good and this friendly.

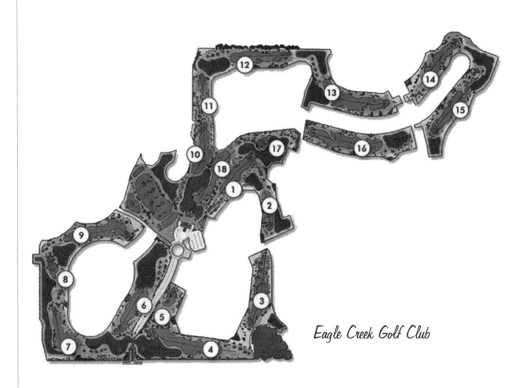

Eagle Creek Golf Club

DEER RIDGE GOLF COURSE

900 Comfort Plaza Dr.

Bellville

419.886.7090

www.deerridgegc.com

QUALITY INN

1000 Comfort Plaza Dr.

Bellville

419.886.7000

Is there such an animal as a one-day getaway? Of course there is, and some places are better than others. The reasonable reasons for a one-day getaway include (but are not limited to, so don't hesitate to make up your own):

1. Boss having surgery.

2. Good report after colonoscopy.

3. Last kid moved out.

4. Giving the kitchen remodeler room to work.

5. Won the Publishers Clearing House Sweepstakes and want to appear modest.

6. Haven't played since last weekend.

7. New puppy in the house is being house trained.

8. New prescription for eyeglasses.

9. Have to bump up the handicap before the club championship.

10. Latest credit score above 680 (or below 500).

11. Test new irons (or woods, or trouble clubs, or putter, or ball retriever).

12. Went entire month without bouncing a check.

You get the idea. Overnighters are easier to pack for, not so hard on the liver or pancreas, and allow playing the same course twice.

In Bellville is such a getaway. Deer Ridge Golf Course and the

Quality Inn are perfect. Here's how we did it. Arranged tee times for two consecutive days at the course, one in the afternoon and the next one at the crack of dawn. Made a reservation at the hotel.

That's it. The hotel is just across the street from the course, so no time is spent traveling from the shower to the first tee.

Deer Ridge Golf Course, another design by the very talented Brian Huntley, is bold and shapely, and worthy of playing consecutive days. He took property that was woods and farm and discovered a course that is alternately confounding and rewarding. Four sets of tees here: black, blue, white, and gold. It's bent grass from the tips to the greens.

It's well-named, too: plenty of deer are in the woods, dodging our slices and hooks and sharing space with foxes, rabbits, and wild turkey. The ridges compete with valleys, hills, plateaus, of the most natural sort. It is one of many Ohio courses where we say, "If the golf cart hadn't been invented, we'd have llamas carrying our sticks."

It is the sort of course, with its dramatic changes in elevation, that leads us to overclub going down and underclub going up. Well, that's the first round. When we tee it up for the second round, we know so much more.

What's more exhilarating, more inspiring, more beautiful than an elevated tee box looking down on Mother Nature's best stuff? That's No. 2, a short par 4 of 245 yards from the blues, with the green clearly in sight. 'Course it's a dogleg right and sand protects the green, but from this tee box, guys whose best drives go 175 think they can get on without wasting time in the fairway. They think wrong. No. 8 is more of the same and the green is 180 feet below the tee. If we would have packed stopwatches, we could have made bets on hang time.

On the back side, No. 16 is memorable because with a great drive, the green looks like an eagle's nest. Of course by this time, we know whose driving game is accurate and whose isn't. It calls for a truly great drive because the landing area is narrow. Plus, it's one of many holes here that are such a pleasure to play, you don't want to get so upset that you can't enjoy it. This course is a great destination regardless of the season, though it's so impressive in the fall that management could start a Fall Festival Tour.

We stayed at the **Quality Inn**, so close you could jog from the room to the first tee. Well, some of us could. The entrance to the course is pretty much all uphill. This getaway being a quick hitter, we didn't spend much time at the hotel, though the time we spent was very, very comfortable. Couldn't guess it from the outside, but the lobby, with its use of rugs and stairway banisters, is elegant. A seating area, with upholstered furniture, is especially well done, because it creates an intimate corner for conversation.

We didn't spend much time at the hotel because we had dinner at the course. The Sand Wedge Grill is not your typical course snack bar, not by any means. It's just four years old, 12,000 square feet, and can comfortably handle as many as 300 guests, so if you find a wedding party there, don't be surprised. Don't compete for the bride's bouquet, either. Hours are 11 in the morning to 9 p.m.

Full service bar, of course, and the Grill's reputation among locals is sterling. That's why it's open year round. They do a stellar job with pastas and beef, so here's a little more scheduling information: Play the first round, have dinner at the club. Shower and sleep (do you believe we didn't have time for cards?), then back to the course for round number two. And before leaving, lunch at the Grill.

And that is the one-night getaway. You'll know it was perfect when you wake the next morning in your own bed and wonder, "Did I just dream that?"

The PGA Junior Championship

Just as the previous generation presented us with golf, complete with instructions, used clubs and shag balls, and places to play, we have an obligation to do the same for the next generation.

The support can come in any number of ways. Maybe we donate used clubs to a muni course teaching kids. It could be keeping a caddy program up and running. Or chipping in for the caddy scholarship programs. Maybe it's taking the gangly kid and his best friend to a short and easy course and teaching golf etiquette. Teaching what we know about the game and its history is something many of us do. In other words, we do what we can.

Cary Blair, now retired, was in a position to do something special for golf. Very special. He was the Big Kahuna at Westfield Insurance, in Westfield Center. He talked the Board of Directors at Westfield Insurance into hosting the PGA Junior Championship, one of golf's most prestigious junior tournaments. The tournament had a seven-year run at Westfield before moving on. A grace note; he brought the 2004 Junior Ryder Cup to Westfield for one of its biennial championships.

Blair had a few things going for him. His company had a long history with golf. (His best on the South Course is 69.) Also two very good golf courses, Westfield North and South. When Geoffrey Cornish built the first one, in 1939, television was a dream. When he built the second, in 1969, the vast wasteland called television was well seeded and growing.

That may have been one of the reasons Blair wanted golf's best young players in Ohio. He and his wife have reared two children. Getting to know and develop friendships with the young players and their parents likely assured the couple that the future was in good hands. Some of the lines on Blair's face come from smiling so much at these tournaments.

In addition to the golf courses, the company has lodging on site for visiting corporate personnel. For the tournaments, the players stayed there, getting to know each other. Here's a thoughtful twist: The parents were not invited to stay with the kids. Parents stayed in area hotels.

The PGA laid out the championship course and roped fairways, stands for galleries, and sent the same PGA rule officials who work the PGA Championship and Ryder Cup events.

And more than that. The boys and girls had fun. At every tournament, each was warmly welcomed by Blair and at the end of play, presented gifts enough to compete with birthday parties. Another twist: Blair had presents for the parents, too. The kids, free from their parents in the evening, got to know each other, develop friendships and see who was best at the video games.

Outside the ropes, parents and friends followed the players. Queried about the quality of the tournament, the answer was always a variation on, "This is the best ever."

No surprise. The residents of Westfield Township and company employees loved the idea; nearly 300 volunteers jumped on board. They directed parking, handed out pairing sheets, served concessions, solicited sponsors, picked up litter, worked as scorers, marshaled galleries and maintained the huge leaderboard. The grounds crew rose to the occasion, daily manicuring the greens on the South course, fluffing sand, repairing divots, and cutting new hole positions.

They did everything except relax and watch the future stars play golf. Lots of players we watch today prepped at this tournament: Tiger and Lefty, Dottie Pepper and Sara Brown, Sean O'Hair and Ryan Moore, among them. Ascending stars that played Westfield include: Michelle Wie, Angela Park, In-Bee Park, Ty Tryon, sisters Arie and Naree Song, and brothers Tony and Gipper Finau.

When Michelle Wie played here, one of her tee shots on No. 10 was an impressive miss. It is a big, rambling, dogleg left, a par 5 with sand dunes and native grasses in the elbow. She failed to put enough draw on the ball and knocked it straight. Into a lake that rarely comes into play. More than 300 yards away. Whew.

In 2007, Alexis Thompson took home the Patty Berg Trophy. She was 12 years old. In spring of 2010, she went 4-0-1 in the Curtis Cup and turned pro. At 15. You can look it up.

Qualifying for this tournament brings the best players in the nation. There are 41 PGA sections in the country, and each section sent its champion boy and girl. There were also a handful of special invitations. The field was 120 players.

Not only did the young champions show up, sponsors and crowds showed up, too. One year more than 10,000 fans went through the gates. (Think about the porta-potty brigade.) And sponsors found great value, too, more than five dozen of them, nearby Smucker's, Pepsi Cola, and Davey Tree among them. Another twist: Enterprise Car Rental provided courtesy cars for the parents. On the side doors were placards announcing the tournament. Some parents, declining the offer and using their own cars, asked Enterprise for door signs to put on their own car doors.

Media coverage, both local and national, made Westfield Center bigger than it was: Population, just a shade over 1,000. After the tournaments, Westfield invited members of the media for a tournament and cookout. Safe to say the scores recorded by the championship players were not in any danger.

Seven consecutive years of being host and title sponsor. For Blair, his days started well before the sun rose and ended long after the sun had set. Talk about a successful and confident field marshal, Blair is it. Wonderful memories and stories he has, but the best is found in his mailbox. At Christmas, a number of players write, wish him a Merry Christmas, and thank him again for the Westfield Junior PGA Championship.

LONGABERGER GOLF CLUB

One Long Dr.
Nashport
740.763.1100
www.longabergergolfclub.com

THE PLACE OFF THE SQUARE

50 North Second St.
Newark
740.322.6455

We have courses named after birds (Quail Hollow), weather (Thunder Hill), Indians (Manakiki), trades (Sawmill and Quarry), jewels (Black Diamond), trees (Oak Shadows), PGA Tour players (Cook's Creek), and hats (Tam O'Shanter).

Longaberger is named for a basket.

Ah, basket-weaving, the apocryphal course of study for Big Ten linemen. In truth, great baskets take great skill and digital dexterity, not an assumed talent of a pulling guard. But a Longaberger basket is not just any basket. Great baskets also call for an eye for art, devotion to quality and—in the case of Longaberger—great marketing.

That describes the golf course designed here by Arthur Hills—an eye for art, a devotion to quality, and great marketing. (The basket company's office is a seven-story basket, a sight unnerving to people not expecting it. They worry that Mighty Joe Young might be on a picnic.)

Longaberger Golf Club just turned 10 years old and it is that rare course that gets demonstrably better with age. A meticulous and professional staff cares for the course and its players like your mother used to care for her roses.

At some tournaments, the starter, when introducing the players at the first tee, reads off a list of their championships. That's a good way to introduce Longaberger: *Golf Digest* said it was the "Best New Upscale Course" in the country when it opened; it has been as high as No. 34 on *Golf Magazine's* "Top 100 You Can Play," *Golfweek* has genuflected a number of times and referred to it as the "Best Public Golf Course in Ohio," among other distinctions.

When the basket company decided to build a golf course, it went first class. The terrain, all 350 acres of gently rolling farmland, was a rough diamond plopped in the lap of one of America's great designers, Ohioan Arthur Hills. He had the soft up-and-down of the farms along with marshland, open fields, and ponds. Hills is a modest man, yet a designer so accomplished in the ways of course creation that many golfers would chip in if a shrine to him were planned.

After Hills finished his work, Longaberger could stretch to 7,243 yards, par 72. Whew.

So, is it really that good? Worth all that hype? Should we make tee times?

In a word: Yup.

It is worth all that hype and maybe a little more because a basket company in the middle of Ohio decided to invest in a golf course and to that end, went flat out: great designer, terrific property, meticulous maintenance, professional and well-trained staff, and a devotion to the Royal and Ancient.

This hypothetical question was bandied about: Given the choice of a free membership at Firestone CC and paying daily fees at Longaberger, which would we take? Hands down it was Longaberger. The pride at Longaberger hasn't yet turned to the hubris at Firestone; Longaberger is a fantastic celebration of golf (please cue up Aaron Copland's "Fanfare for the Common Man") and Firestone is a fantastic celebration of country club life. Golf is played for lots of reasons at Firestone and other, similar private clubs, where golf is first a measure of social and business success. Golf at Longaberger is played for the unsullied joy of the game.

We got this advice from a fellow trunk-slammer who was familiar with the course, and while it sounded a bit wacko, we followed it and will always be glad we did: change tee boxes as the game goes on. That is, if it was clear that the tee presented a hole we were clearly not going to par, we stepped up. On most par 3s, we went to the waybacks just for the fun of it. Sometimes back, sometimes middle, sometimes in-between (there are five sets of tees). We're well aware we couldn't submit this score for our handicap, but it allowed us to prepare well for the second round, a true practice round, as it were. Later, over beers in the clubhouse, it occurred to us we played faster by changing tees. And when we played our second round, we better understood the course.

That change-the-tee idea made the first hole playable. It's an uphill par 4, 411 from the waybacks and features a sharp dogleg with bunkers in the elbow. Not the hole you want to card a six or seven.

Water is in play on only six holes, greens are well guarded with bunkers, including our personal favorites, grass bunkers. Do we have to say that after ten years, these gorgeous greens have settled? If you have the right line, hit it and don't worry.

Hope the swooning is over by the fourth tee because this par 5 begins from an elevated tee and calls for restraint and respect: If you can restrain from over swinging and play it as the three-shot hole it is, the green becomes accessible. From the tee, you're going to hit down 135 feet; your hang time will be far better than OSU punter Jon Thoma's. The green is small and the Swiss Guards couldn't guard it any better: water, rocks, scary sand and a ravine.

Howzabout a short par 4? Always a design challenge, and success might be measured by the number of players who unwittingly assume a birdie and then walk off with worse than par. No. 11 is a brief 364 and that's from the tips.

A friend of ours used to say melancholy washed over him at the seventeenth tee because he knew that after the seventeenth was the final hole.

We think he would feel despair at the thought of finishing his round, but absolutely exhilarated to play the home hole. In the distance stands the baronial clubhouse and before us is spread a long par 4, beginning with an elevated tee and a fairway that falls and rises like a hammock.

We camped at Longaberger's **The Place Off The Square**, in Newark, but had dinner at the club. Grouper with mashed red skins and asparagus. Beer is the only proper accompaniment. Also a pork filet. Both excellent and we enjoyed the service: very professional, yet friendly. The room is big and handsome, the windows perfect for gazing away, and portions big enough we passed on dessert. That's big.

We would have taken more notes, but after an hour on the driving range, half hour on the putting green, four hours on the course, well, a man only has so much energy. The Place is not a Longaberger original; the company bought it, kept the indoor pool, outfitted it with lots and lots of baskets and opened the doors to 117 rooms and while it will benefit from a renovation, it was more than adequate.

How nice to come home as basket cases.

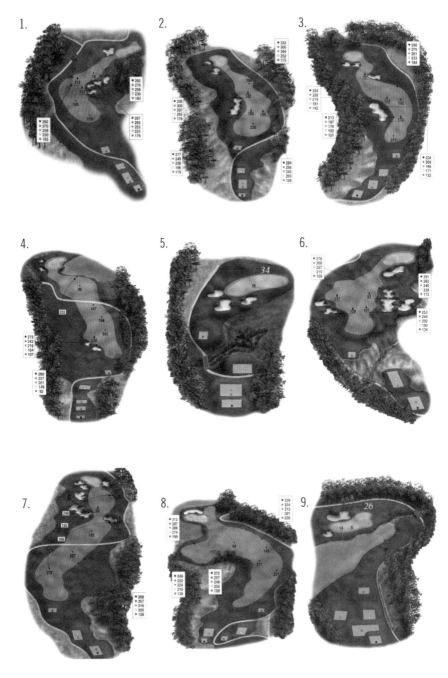

Longaberger

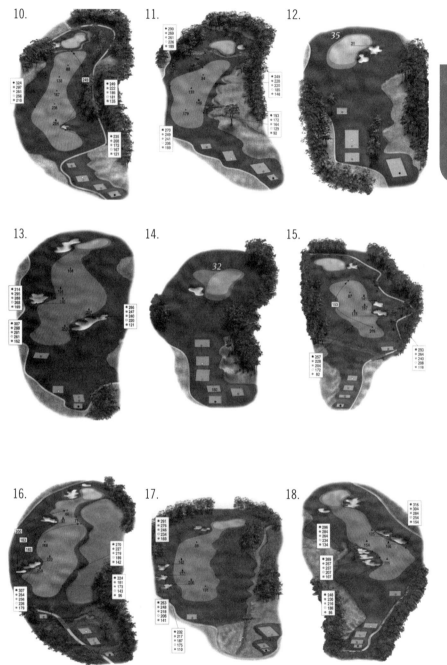

Coupon Golf

Tee Time Golf Pass
800-444-9203
www.TeeTimeGolfPass.com

We wonder if the greatest obstacle to golf travel will be the baggage fees charged by airlines. Although when it comes to obstacles, take your pick:

1. Arriving two hours before your flight is scheduled, so you can be patted down by a federale before being herded, like fattened hogs, into seats designed to stuff more of us in.
2. Ticket prices. Like your handicap, they ain't going down.
3. Renting cars, and listening to the scary spiel about the need for extra insurance, plus getting it back on time with sufficient gasoline.
4. Traffic in a resort town.
5. The one we hate the most comes from Myrtle Beach—surcharges. Suddenly having a surcharge added to the green fees makes the golf package no bargain. Plus, they know they

have us by the golf balls.

We'll be happy if any one of those five or any combination thereof gives pause. (We also disliked arriving at the home airport, tired as sled dogs, and having to retrieve the sticks and luggage and get a ride home.) Ever occur to you that the two hours of pat down before each flight and who knows how long to retrieve baggage, equals way more than four hours? Enough for 18 holes?

Hope so, because it will keep more of us in Ohio. After a season of all-Ohio golf, you become a convert. In the future, trips that call for air transport or crossing state lines are no longer attractive.

You think of the fried perch at Brennans, the grandeur of the first tee at Black Diamond, shooting pool into the wee hours at the historic Marriott Inn in downtown Cleveland, playing courses designed by Tom Weiskopf and John Cook, Brian Huntley and Arthur Hills, Hurdzan and Fry, and Donald Ross.

The memories won't stop there. We fell in love with playing in college towns. The State Park resorts with great courses and, bless their hearts, cottages. If cottages weren't built for golf, poker, and whiskey, we are purely baffled.

Okay, back to airline fuel surcharges, golf course surcharges, car rental fees and the rest. In Ohio, we have a golf savings plan that might work wonders for your wallet. It worked miracles on ours. You know the entertainment coupon books? The ones that have two-for-one deals at everything from oil changes to hamburger joints? And some golf courses, too, all local. Used properly, they can save money.

The same idea, with a number of improvements, was incorporated for an Ohio golf book. It's called *Tee Time Golf Pass* and it costs $45. It's brochure form, 70-some pages, fits in the side pocket of a golf bag (or in the glove compartment) and the only addition we made was a plastic sandwich bag—that's what we kept it in to protect it from the elements.

We like the program for a few reasons. First, it works. Well, it works for us. If you play only your regular course and rarely venture out, it's not for you. On the other hand, if your golf anthem is "On the Road Again," this thing is found money. Second, it covers the waterfront. In the front is a list of the courses. Here is a sample, a baker's dozen: Atwood Lake, Aurora, Black Diamond, Blue Heron, Chapel Hills, Chippewa, Cook's Creek, Cumberland, Eagle Sticks, Fowler's Mill, Granville, Grey Hawk, Legends of Massillon, Little Mountain, Longaberger, Manakiki, Maumee Bay, Oak Shadows, Mill Creek, Pine Hills, Red Hawk, Reserve Run, Sanctuary, Shaker Run, Tam O'Shanter, Thunder Hill, The Quarry, Windmill Lakes, Windy Knoll. A few more than thirteen; arithmetic was never a strength.

Here's how it works. When you call for a tee time, you tell them you're a member of Tee Time Golf Pass. Show up at the cashier's counter, sign up and pay for a cart (all courses charge for carts; what the heck, they have to make a few bucks).

Here are two examples. You show up at New Albany Links, it costs you $15 for the riding cart and ... well, that's it. The free round is a one-trick pony, but the next two times you show up, it's only $27.

You show up at Windy Knoll and

hand your brochure to the cashier. Total cost is $12. We are not kidding.

The brochure lists the deals. Maybe at one course, the first use is a free round. Second time you go is one paid, one free. Third time you go might be one paid and one free, or one free and three paid.

Good thing about the brochure is you see exactly what you're going to get. Cart fees are listed, too. Don't have to clip coupons and put them in your wallet. At the course, they'll mark what you just used. Most courses have a series of deals.

This book has other, vital features we like. First, it isn't new. It was started in 1993. Started small; still growing. Two hundred seventy-two Ohio courses so far.

One of the company's two core values is: We exist to glorify God through the tithe of our profit. To which we say, Amen, brother.

GRANVILLE GOLF COURSE
555 Newark-Granville Rd.
Granville
740.587.GOLF (4653)
www.granvillegolf.com

GRANVILLE INN
314 E. Broadway
Granville
740.587.3333
888.472.6855

CHERRY VALLEY LODGE
2299 Cherry Valley Rd.
Newark
740.788.1200
800.788.8008

Now here's a selling point about Ohio golf getaways: Playing courses put together by golf's late, great designers as well as the very best of the new generation.

Enter Donald Ross, the pride of Dornoch, Scotland, whose work in the U.S., in the first half of the twentieth century, will always impress and challenge us.

Want proof? **Granville Golf Course** was built eighty-five years ago. More proof? Dornoch's favorite son designed Pinehurst No. 2 and Seminole. In Ohio, Mill Creek and Manakiki are open to trunk-slammers. Inverness and Scioto are among his private tracks.

Talk about your prolific, Ross designed more than 400 U.S. courses. You give this guy a topo map and he could see a golf course that needed only routing, bunkers, and greens.

While Ross was searching the properties for natural hazards and design features, golf clubs were undergoing the biggest change in the history of the Royal and Ancient: steel shafts. That meant out with hickory shafts and clubs named niblick, cleek, mashie, and jigger, and in with the 1-2-3-4-5-6-7-8-9-irons. Baffies became 5-woods and spoons became 3-woods. A 2-wood replaced the brassie. Suddenly, breaking a club over one's knee became more hazardous; hickory breaks much easier than steel.

This course with the innocuous name isn't long, even from the way backs: 6,559 yards, par 71, course rating of 71.3, slope 128. Course rating and slope say it all.

In the clubhouse, they brag about some of the better players who have teed it up here, including Gene Sarazen, Walter Hagen, and Horton Smith. You can be the fourth and play with the ghosts of the game.

When Granville was built, there were no shapers on bulldozers, which will surprise first-timers. The use of elevation, canted fairways and multi-tiered greens were a matter of Mother Nature or a team of oxen.

The fun begins with a brief, 334-yard, par 4, and men wiser than us in the ways of golf reach for a fairway wood or long iron on the first tee.

A long track? Not hardly. A tough track? Most assuredly. There are more than five dozen sand traps here, some with stiff upper lips. Enough fairways are canted and suddenly, hook lie and slice lie become important considerations. Plenty of changes in elevation, and we decided that playing one's best round here wouldn't be until the fifth or sixth tour around the course. There is that much to think about between tee and cup.

The use of elevation, canted fairways and multi-tiered greens were a matter of Mother Nature or a team of oxen.

Trees line No. 1 and it's easy to see where the ball should go. This hole is the Granville introduction to sloped fairways, protective bunkers, and elevated greens.

'Kay, warmed up? Good, because No. 2 is one of the best holes here, and on the tee, time to unload the big lumber. Just getting from tee to fairway is long. There's water on this hole and the approach is to an elevated, sand-protected, multi-tiered green. Walking off with a bogey is cause for shouts of, "Good hole!"

Some par 4s play long; some play short. This one plays long, regardless of tee. Water, trees, and a green so high you'll need a shot of oxygen before reading the green. It doesn't stop there; a two-tiered green is waiting. Holy Moly!

No. 5, a dogleg par 4 is interesting because club pro Rodney Butt grew up just a 7-iron away. He's also one of the golf coaches at the high school and at Denison University.

The par 5s here are almost always three-shotters, though tempting for players who have the length and buccaneer blood.

Knowledge of risk and reward. It isn't that the par 5s here are so long; it's that launching the approach calls for a truly inspired shot. So the reward is there, but we never found it to be equal to the risk. No. 10 is a good example: An uphill tee shot to a steeply sloping fairway. What, you're going to launch your best shot of the day from a seriously unlevel lie?

Twenty-some years ago, new owners of the course added housing and in order to do what they wanted, four holes were relocated and redesigned in keeping with Ross's style. A good job was done; it never occurred to us to say, "This doesn't fit here."

There are homes now, of course, and homes are often a distraction to players. Maybe not so much here; the homes are McMansions and an interesting sight to behold. Not as interesting as getting around this course, but interesting.

For all the beauty of the course, it's the home hole that stays with us. The view from the tee box is one that can be aptly described as a picture worth a thousand words. A par 4 from an elevated tee, in the distance we see the town and the church spires. And standing on this high tee box, the green within view (and reach, some of us think), high hopes trump judgment. Lesser and greater men believed the green to be reachable.

Fools rush in.

Sand dots both sides of the fairway and trees make it a hallway. Slicing or hooking here means the next shot is a low punch just to get back in play, and who practices drawing or fading a low punch shot?

Played properly, on the other hand, means that when head hits pillow and the events of the day are reviewed, that eighteenth hole is played over and over, never losing its sweetness.

And speaking of heads colliding with pillows, there are two distinct places to stay in Granville, one an inn and the other a lodge. Both offer golf packages. In the interest of readers, we stayed one night at the Granville Inn, played the course and then spent another night at Cherry Valley Lodge and played the course a second time. (We scored higher on the second round. Go figure.)

The Granville Inn was built in 1923 and is on the National Register of Historic Places. The Tudor manor has fewer than thirty rooms, and they aren't big. They are comfortable, and blessed with antique furniture that works, hand-crafted woodwork, a proud staff and very good restaurant. Plus, the Inn has Granville, a small town that is dignified, true to its New England heritage, and as far as we're concerned, the best town for ambling along after dinner, a hand-rolled double corona in hand. In spite of growth, some welcome and some not welcome, the flavor and charm remain. Settling on a bench and watching the world go by reminded us, what was our hurry?

The restaurant at the Inn includes a pub and patio. When the weather gets chilly, propane heaters are lighted.

Don't dawdle. The restaurant closes at 9 p.m. When we're on a getaway, we're of a mind to sit down for supper around 7 p.m. For the first time in a long time, we ordered frog legs and wondered why more restaurants don't offer them. (And no, they don't taste like chicken; they taste like frogs.) Those tender little thighs and calves were fried perfectly, and so delicately flavored we never reached for the tartar sauce. A pork chop and spaetzel sounds like a comfort dish your Aunt Louise served you. Not to start an argument, but this is better. Finding a pork chop this thick, yet this tender, is always worthy of remark. For those who know how to order and enjoy, there's a good wine list here, too.

The Cherry Valley Lodge is on the border of town, and it takes a more modern tack. It was built on an eighteen-acre lot and until one of our group strolled the grounds, we forgot how much pleasure some guys take in their gardens.

Here's an honor reserved for a very few: the American Public Gardens Association lauds the greenery. And it's easy to enjoy because among the 2,000 plantings and 400 species in the Arboretum & Botanical Garden, most are labeled.

Back up just a bit. Can't talk about the place without first mentioning walking in to the place, and being struck by the huge fireplaces. Invariably, we were told, first timers immediately tilt their heads back to take in the grandeur. (Did we say grandeur? In a golf book? Well, yes, we did. That's our story and we're sticking to it.)

In addition to the gardens, there is a huge indoor water park, including a heated pool for those sore muscles. A spa is there, but we didn't investigate. Half-court roundball can be played if you have more energy than good sense. And if a postprandial promenade is part of your routine, the country pathways here are perfect (birders take note). Another pleasure is peace and quiet. At night we heard only Mother Nature.

Rooms here are handsome and comfortable, but we didn't spend much time in them till we ate. There are 200 rooms here, and the suite is perfect for poker. Every comfort and convenience except a cigaret girl. The restaurant, equally handsome and comfortable, is our favorite. The layout makes it appear more club like than it actually is.

There doesn't appear to be a dress code, but your mother would be scandalized if you sat down wearing shorts, tee shirt and flip flops. In any restaurant, dress should match the amenities. Or, as our Aunt Louise told us, many years ago, if the place has white tablecloths, we were to show up in white shirts.

The restaurant offers an old-fashioned salad, one many people are unfamiliar with: the wedge. It is a quarter head of lettuce and here it is served with blue cheese dressing, bacon, tomatoes and chopped egg. A Caesar is on the menu, but unless it comes with raw egg and anchovies, we demur.

The steak salad we enjoyed and ordered it because it's a flat iron steak with luscious beefsteak tomatoes and gorgonzola. We never got to the entrees; our salads were perfect. But they do sound tempting for the next trip. One plate has crab, shrimp, and sea scallops finished off with a lobster sauce. Talk about your picking up everything on the sea floor. All grass fed steaks are here and some good-looking pasta plates. Ah, so little time, so many decisions.

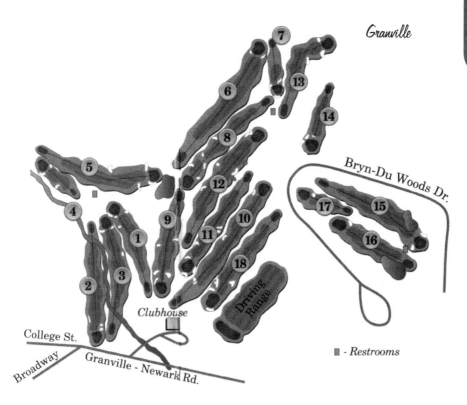

Granville

Bryn-Du Woods Dr.

Clubhouse

Driving Range

College St.

Broadway

Granville - Newark Rd.

■ - *Restrooms*

DEER CREEK STATE PARK
20635 State Park Rd. 20
Mt. Sterling
740.869.3124
www.deercreekstateparklodge.com

Too bad venison is an acquired taste. If the fast food joints sold venison burgers instead of beef (or what passes for it), the golf community would provide free branding. If you were playing at **Deer Creek State Park**, wouldn't it suggest, however subliminally, that after a round, you enjoy a venison taco, or venison weenie, or pizza with venison sausage, or the best of all, the Double Bambi Burger and instead of salt shakers, have salt licks on every table?

We discussed this important question after noticing how many golf courses were named for *odocoileus virginianus*. They include, but are not limited to: Deer Ridge, Deer Run, Deer Pass, Deer Track, and Deer Creek. The only one missing is Deer John.

Deer Creek State Park shares many virtues with the rest of the state parks that offer golf. All courses are maintained well, eminently playable, terrific values, and staffed by friendly people. The friendliness of the staffs may be because almost all are locals; they know not only the park, but the surrounding area, too. We found them happy to brag about their home towns. An unheralded treat: no housing developments on the courses.

Maybe best of all, for golf getaway purposes, they have cottages. Cottages put lots of space between us and other guests. It means we can step out for a smoke, drink beer from the bottle, tell jokes we would never tell in mixed company, play cards all night, and not put too much emphasis on fastidiousness, personal hygiene, or good manners.

A half dozen guys can be comfortable in the cottages here, more if they're related. Everything is furnished and extras included are television and natural gas fireplaces. Porches are screened in, which is the best defense against mosquitoes, but they are also the best seat in the house when a summer storm rolls across Pickaway County.

The course here can play as long as 7,113 yards, and par is 71. Big hitters are welcomed, watched, and admired; trees are not tall enough to produce ricochets. Yet. The course rating is 73.7, enough to make most of us back away. The course has only been open since 1983, and was designed by Jack Kidwell. Greens are bent and fairways are blue. The driving range and putting green are yours before you tee it up. Four sets of tees here and even ours, the whites, had length: 6,600 yards. The number of ponds surprised us: ten of them. The surprise came when we found them. Between the water, fifty-two sand traps and trees, this essentially flat course, with a few gentle rolls, is challenging and satisfying.

There are two of our all-time favorite hazards here, grass bunkers, which can make a vicar curse. If you tumble in, pitch out, and make par, we know you have a short game. There are more doglegs here than at your local kennel, which we found to be a good way to make a flat course interesting. Both fades and draws worked, but hooks and slices? Nada. In the elbows are sand bunkers.

We made the course play better with our Tips Rule: on par 3s and 5s, we go all the way back to tee it up. That meant for the par 5s, yardages were: 508, 575, 549, 567 yards. Except for the fourth par 5, all were more than 500 even from the whites.

In retrospect, we shouldn't have done that on the par 3s. There are six of them. No. 3 is darn near 200 yards to a two-tiered green; No. 11 has sand in front and water left, forest behind. No. 15 has grasses down the right, and pond and bunker on the left. You get the idea. Bogeys are penciled in far more often than pars.

We think the signature hole should be No. 12, a long par 4 with a narrow fairway. A good drive takes advantage of gravity for some extra yardage, and that's good, because the approach from the 150 yard marker is uphill and the shot can call for as much as a two-club difference. Furthermore, left of the green is sand and forest. The forest is so close we thought we'd find deer droppings on one of the pin positions.

The lodge combines rusticity with modernity, using lots of stone and wood and plenty of windows. Every state park has its natural beauty, and this is no exception. Over the course of a lot of holes, lots of dinners and drinks, some very comfortable lodgings at some great prices, we wonder: Is the state park system one of Ohio's great unsung virtues?

The topic came up while dining at Rafter's, the restaurant here. Maybe it was inspired by the view. Big, tall windows right on Deer Creek Lake was part of it and the service was another and the food still another. It was the cynic at our table who got us started when he observed the many families enjoying dinner and the hard-working staff smiling. Government employees, he said. Look at all the government employees smiling and so are the taxpayers they're serving. There is some political hay to be made here. He said if the turnpike commission operated as well as the Ohio Department of Natural Resources, Ohio would be increasing its population. (See Hueston Woods.)

Whatever it is, it's done well. Here's the surprise: When we asked dozens of friends and drinking partners if they had taken advantage of the park system, few had. Fewer still knew of the nearby fun to be had.

Of course most of them were city slickers, which brings us to another idea from the cynic. He says, and we believe, that the revolution in golf equipment technology is nice, but the greatest assist to golf is the interstate highway system. Really? Yes, he said. Think about it: we get to play great and different courses all over the state because getting there, which used to be half the battle, is a snap. His closing was equally provocative. He said the overwhelming majority of golfers never break 90, despite drivers with club heads the size of wheel blocks, shafts made in chemist's labs, and balls so ready to go that the USGA is always thinking about limiting their horsepower. A few years ago, PGA professional Mike Mural, who was named "Teacher of the Year" by the Northern Ohio PGA, put it best: "New materials help, but if you don't have a swing, the ball really doesn't care if it's hit with a persimmon driver or a moon rock. It still ain't going to go where you want."

Back to Rafter's. Dress is casual, and on Sunday mornings, beginning at 9, the buffet opens. Man, if there is a more satisfying way to eat well, eat lots, and enjoy brunch, we don't know where to look. There is a downside, and that is settling into the cart, groaning, and announcing, "I don't remember the last time I had thirds." (Take this guy's bet.)

Deer Creek

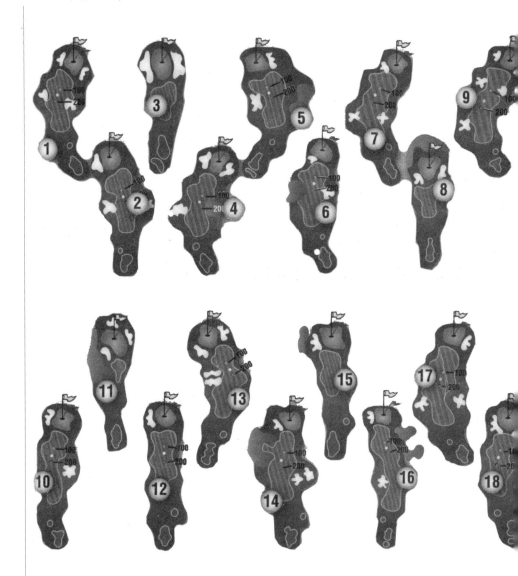

REASONS WHY WOMEN AREN'T INVITED TO GOLF GETAWAYS

The best lessons in golf are provided by Tour players, and not the PGA Tour, but the LPGA Tour. The sweetest, softest swings are to be found here. If most over-swinging guys could imitate those swings, the world would be a much better place.

That doesn't mean we'll include women on getaways. Here are the reasons women are not invited to golf getaways.

1. Women rate golf courses by the number and variety of flower beds.

2. On women's golf bags is what looks like a string of worry beads. It is a device by which they can count their strokes.

3. Their toiletries and beauty equipment weigh more than their golf bags.

4. The day before a getaway, they bake stuff and bring it along.

5. They dress every bit as well as members of the LPGA Tour. They often offer non sequiturs to each other such as, "Oh, that ties it all together."

6. Their betting limits are ten cents.

7. They yell stuff like, "That's not fair," and ask questions such as, "I don't have to count that as a stroke, do I?"

8. If shopping is not included in the getaway, they become moody.

9. They consistently draw to inside straights.

10. True story. Rev. George Hrbek, a veteran of getaways, sometimes takes his wife to a local course. Last summer, on a par 4, she hit a couple nice shots and was left with a wedge to the green. Her third shot bounced into the cup. She immediately drew her cell phone and called friends to tell them about it.

ROYAL AMERICAN LINKS
3300 Miller Paul Rd.
Galena
740.965.1215
www.royalamericanlinks.com

BENT TREE GOLF CLUB
350 Bent Tree Rd.
Sunbury
740.965.5140
www.benttreegc.com

Boy, talk about your contradictions in terms. There isn't anything royal in this country. A couple centuries ago, we made sure of that. And in Ohio, the pounding heart of American golf, there are no links courses. The closest we have come to royalty and golf is the late Payne Stewart, who was called, behind his back, a royal Payne. But no crown. No ermine.

The closest we come to links courses are empty parking lots at supermarkets: hard, fast, with hidden traps of all sorts, no trees or bushes.

That doesn't mean **Royal American Links** should be bypassed on the Golf Tour of Life. Just the opposite. Great course with a regrettable name, that's all.

Maybe the primary reason for the beauty and challenge of the course is Michael Hurdzan, designer. Handing over to him a couple hundred acres is like turning over your capital building fund to I.M. Pei. In both cases, the men are artisans and artists, and their work will last long after we bury them.

From the waybacks, it isn't long, 6,800 yards. But Hurdzan uses water, mounds, sand, pot bunkers, and his wonderful wizardry with greens to make it what it is. All that and Hurdzan is one of the best when it comes to incorporating drama. Lots of his holes, seen from the tee box for the first time, appear to have been painted on the landscape. That's the sensual drama. The drama in the game is two-fold. First, winning players on his courses are golf strategists who keep ego under control. Second, with Hurdzan courses, there's no coasting; it ain't over until it's over. Add to that bent grass throughout and course maintenance of the first order.

From the whites, it plays just a bit over 6,400 yards and both sides start with par 5s. Mmmm. No. 1, 518 yards, plays perfectly for two-digit handicaps as well as guys who can properly aim and control their howitzers. Hurdzan made sure that if that heroic 3-wood shot was coming in, the green would be deep enough to slow and hold the shot. Somebody say eagle on the first hole?

In other words, you leave ego at the cart barn and you'll love it.

Hurdzan uses marshland and other wet spots to amp up the natural beauty, and like all his courses, he allows you to understand what the hole calls for, but he depends on your judgment and course management skills to score well. In other words, you leave ego at the cart barn and you'll love it.

Two virtues: It isn't long and it is walkable. Few guys on getaways walk, and that's a shame. The beauty of a course can't be appreciated from a riding cart. Here's something we started doing and it works well. Designate a driver who will allow his partner to walk. This means keeping an eye on the walker and deliver clubs to him in a timely manner. But the guy who is walking suddenly understands what private club players have long enjoyed: someone else hauling the bag around. The arrangement can be reversed at the turn. One more thing here: no castles or other residential development.

It is essentially a flat course, so you know Hurdzan is going to challenge our wedges, sand wedges, and putters.

No. 3 is one of the designer's par 4s where he finished it and walked away with a smile, thinking, "From the tee, it's looks difficult. That would be because it is."

Handsome, two-story clubhouse here and if you can't wait to win back money lost on the course, this is a pretty nice place to shuffle and deal. The place bears a striking resemblance to Balmoral. Except for Old Glory on the flagpole. It's more like a private club and better than some private clubs. Very good food, too.

We loved what the pro told us. He does it all for guys like us on getaways. He works with hotels, makes tee times—this guy will even recommend and make reservations for dinner.

Small hotel, big rooms. More handsome than your picture in the yearbook. Might be the most spacious rooms we enjoyed. Small bar off the lobby, too.

The nearby Easton Town Center offers a variety of dining choices including steaks and seafood at Mitchell's Ocean Club, Italian favorites at Brio and the renowned Smith and Wollensky chain.

And those who wish to mix in some play on a traditional course can make the short trip down the road to the **Bent Tree Golf Club**. Stretching over 167 acres of naturally wooded, rolling terrain, Bent Tree Golf Club is one of the best championship courses in central Ohio. Designed by Dennis Griffiths, this top rated golf course features bent grass tees, fairways and greens, as well as many bunkers and abundant water.

The generally ample and carefully undulating fairways are often bordered by marshy creeks and lots of wild grassy areas. There are also a good number of holes with thick trees cover and there is plenty water on this course. The bunkering gives nice definition to the layout without being too penal and as usual, Hurdzan's greens and greens complexes are outstanding. The third hole, a shortish par 4, can easily set you back a few holes. From the elevated tee it is visually intimidating because all you see is carry over a large lake to a tight fairway hemmed in by mature trees. There really is no place to miss so hit a precise hybrid or fairway wood here, giving yourself enough club to carry the water. The fifth hole is memorable for a nice effort at a bunker resembling the "church pews." The ninth hole is such a great hole it almost deserves to be the eighteenth. It is one of the four exciting par 5s. Its initial landing area is rather wide but you need some length because the real trouble is the second shot. A large lake occupies the left side of the fairway which must be crossed at some point to approach the green. You can shorten your approach if you deliver a solid fairway, wood into the landing area, which gets wider as it nears the green, or lay up well short but to a tighter fairway. Pick your poison. The eighteenth is an excellent finishing hole in its own right. The well designed par 4 finishing hole requires a long tee shot to a fairly wide fairway or you're looking at over 200 yards to a protected green. Perhaps that is not so bad, but thirty yards short of the green is a marsh which will put pressure on your long game. All things said, you will have a good time on this fine course, which won't beat you up too much. Very good practice facilities and a beautiful clubhouse.

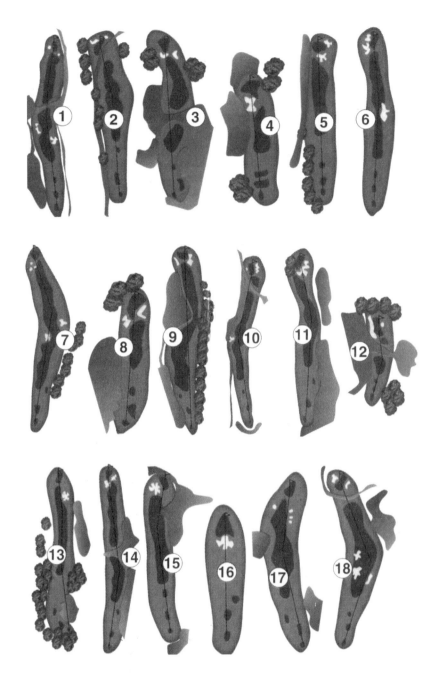

Royal American Links

Parking

Clubhouse

EAST GOLF CLUB
6140 Babbitt Rd.
New Albany
614.855.8600
www.eastgolfclub.com

EMBASSY SUITES COLUMBUS
2700 Corporate Exchange Dr.
Columbus
614.890.8600

RUSTY BUCKET
180 Market St.
New Albany
614.939.5300

And why, you ask, do we want to stay at a place on Corporate Exchange Drive? Isn't the purpose of a getaway to, well, get away? And now we're supposed to share lodging with suits?

Oh, get off your high horse and think for a minute. Luxuriate in the envious stares, the wide-eyed jealousy, when the suits see you, resplendent in Sligo golf pants, (a non-threatening green plaid,) topped with a white Puma pique shirt and the ugly but enviable cap from the Masters. One of us always refers to it as "green bean green." (It is one of those outfits where a woman is *not* going to say, "Oh, yes, the bright green bean green hat pulls it all together.")

You're going to play **East Golf Club**, another Arthur Hills masterpiece, and we're not kidding. The suits are going to sit through a marketing meeting. Or worse, an excited lecture from some guy who bills himself as an inspirational speaker. The suits know that you know and you know that they know. Yes, it's a cheap trick, but we enjoyed it. From breakfast buffet to the first tee is a little under twenty minutes, and here's your lucky charm for the day: you're driving on the Jack Nicklaus Freeway.

And when you arrive at East, you'll forget all about the juvenile, yet amusing, mind games. It won't take long for this course and this club to quickly float to the top of your Top Ten List. Both clubhouse and course are luxurious. It's not easy to say a golf club is flawless, but even if we were as nitpicky as your Aunt Louise, we would have nothing to criticize and much to admire and enjoy.

Arthur Hills, who loves playing golf as much as he loves designing golf courses, sculpted this one in 1991. Under another name (Winding Hollow) it was a private course and club built for the landed gentry, and when they packed up and left in 2007, they left behind all the good stuff. They should have left the name, too, because it describes the course far better.

If we had royalty in this country, they would park their crowns and scepters at this place. An outgoing, proud, and professional staff, a majestic clubhouse, very good food at the Tap-In Lounge, and a course where, once on, it is difficult to leave. No McMansions and no hum of traffic, East is majestic. It is serene and peaceful, far from the Sturm und Drang of city life; precious few are like East. Plenty of water here (on half the holes), and Hills makes it look natural. Plenty of tall, mature trees, too, that he used to frame holes, slow the march to par, and create anxiety attacks for nesting birds. Hills builds very challenging courses, but never are they tricked up. When we were there, the course played fast, actually too fast for us. Given the beauty of the course, we would have enjoyed communing with Ma Nature while the group in front of us slowed to find a lost ball.

If we had royalty in this country, they would park their crowns and scepters at this place.

Playing a first round here elicits a thoughtful post-game reaction, "Hmmm. I want to play again." That is golfspeak for "I demand a rematch."

Let's not kid around; it's often a tight course and leaving Mister

Boom-Boom in the bag is usually the judicious start of a hole. Not for us, though. We played a four-man scramble, planning to finish five or six under, so bad shots were quickly forgotten. Truth to tell: We still didn't break par. (When four tee shots miss the par 3 green, you know you're not going to be collecting prizes.) The longest route is 6,900 yards, and given the accuracy Hills demands, we'll never play those tees. That didn't stop us from walking to the back of the box just to admire what Hills hath wrought.

Back to **Embassy Suites**, on Corporate Exchange Drive, to shower and change. The hotel is bountiful after a $7 million makeover and most of those dollars went to make us more comfortable. In big ways (wait till you pull up the sheets) and little ways (that drape blocks every speck of light from the room). Suites are expertly designed and professionally furnished. It's not just that every amenity is here; it's that at home we don't even have half these amenities.

Want to stay in for dinner? Welcome to the Atrium Grille, a very nice place where informal doesn't mean unprofessional.

In addition to playing head games with suits, there are other, better reasons for staying at the Embassy. It is nothing but suites, 200 of them. Get the poker chips from the trunk of the car, take and deliver drink orders, open a new deck of cards, and say grace. Grace? We have an occasional member who says a sort of grace. He lifts his glass and says, "I'm grateful I'm an American." And that's all he says. But when he says it, he reminds of us how indescribably fortunate we are and each of us takes a minute to reflect. Boy, talk about a way to start a game of Texas Hold 'Em.

Enough of this high end stuff. There is, in New Albany, the **Rusty Bucket.** How could we not go? Deep fried pickles, an Italian sub of frightening proportions, a bucket of chicken wings (or mini-burgers). And our personal favorite, sautéed garlic spinach. Once you taste it, you'll want to have it for breakfast before a match. The Bucket is a chain, but a very good one.

At the Bucket, it's pure casual, so don't worry about racing back to the Embassy to change. Don't be surprised to find students, parents, kids, and lots of guys just like us. It's so easy to say, "Let's go have a beer at the Bucket."

Our table was off to the side and we watched the wait staff zip hither and yon, doing a great imitation of a bee hive. The queen bee was behind those kitchen doors. There were a dozen and half servers, and it seemed they didn't have a low gear. The place can comfortably handle almost 200, and that includes twenty-five or so in a very comfortable bar. We decided the Bucket is "nicely loud," so you can't hear the game on the television sets, but you can hear each other.

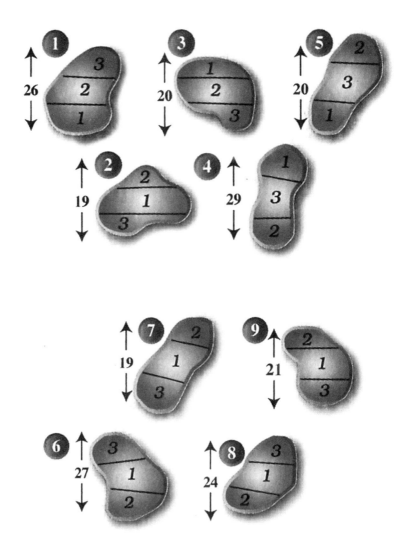

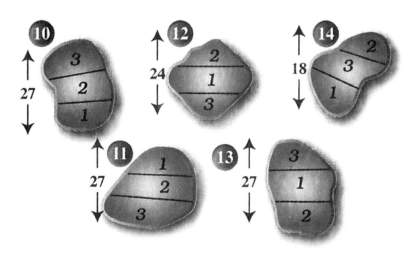

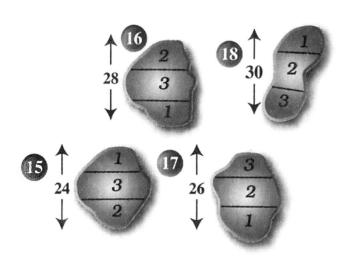

COOK'S CREEK GOLF CLUB

16405 US 23 South
Ashville
740.983.3636
www.cookscreek.com

THE LOFTS
55 Nationwide Blvd.
Columbus
614.461.2663

MAX AND ERMA'S
55 E Nationwide Blvd.
Columbus
614.228.5555

We'd like to play **Cook's Creek Golf Club** once a week, from the beginning of the season till they take down the flags. Talk about your provenance: Hurdzan, Fry and Cook. What Winkin, Blinkin and Nod are to sleeping, these guys are to golf.

Hurdzan/Fry, the Columbus design firm, continues to buff its image creating great courses across the country. Former PGA Tour professional John Cook is now on the old man's tour. A long, tall, blond born-in-Toledo boy (Go, Mud Hens!) and a champion golfer at Ohio State (Go, Bucks!), Cook was part of OSU's 1979 NCAA championship team and he won eleven times on the PGA Tour.

It all begins with a turn into the circular driveway in front of the big, good-looking clubhouse. The course opened in 2004, and while it can play a bit over 7,000 yards, even Cook would have trouble coming in under par. His driving average is around 275, though, we hasten to add, that's in the fairway. What the heck, the course rating from the waybacks is 73.7. Par is 72. Included is a pretty fancy GPS screen on the cart. When you drive where you're not supposed to, the screen yells at you. Not unlike your parents, who used to boom, "Don't make me come up there."

With the Scioto River on the course, irrigation is not a problem.

Matter of fact, the front side rests on a flood plain. Just because a number of holes have water on both sides of the fairway, or wrap around a green, is no reason for you to get your ball retriever regripped.

Most of the time, but not all, the water frames the hole or gives pause before the takeaway. Other times, it will break your heart. Such is golf.

The first time we played the course, we were indiscreet with club selection and—can we say it?—full of ourselves. A couple more rounds here and we were both humble and realistic. And that is when the pleasures of the course presented themselves. Playing a hole well at this course provides the sense of satisfaction most hackers will never know.

Did we say flood plain? That's true, but there's so much more to the terrain here, and The Three Amigos made beautiful use of the hilly, rolling countryside, especially on the back side. Here's a word that rarely comes up with golf courses: balance. But when we talked about the course, we said it has balance and we meant that The Three Amigos had the basics for a good course: water, woods, and changes in elevation. They were able to perfectly balance these three elements.

The grass is bent throughout. No surprise that the superintendent is proud of his greens; to us, they presented the perfect challenge: If you can see the line, the ball will follow it. No excuse for four-putting here.

Big driving range here. If short on time, we recommend warming up the mid-irons; they'll play an important role. Want to know the speed of the greens? Toss a ball on the practice green, watch it roll, pick it up, and report to the first tee.

We added one more compliment when we learned the place is also an Audubon Sanctuary and has a rookery for blue herons. We said, and I quote, "A course for the ages."

Cook's Creek uses the view from No. 15 in lots of its marketing stuff and it's a good choice. From an elevated green, this par 3 of 162 yards from the grays, is glorious. It's a peninsula green and anchored on the far right with a tall tree. The green seduces with a soft voice, "Well, of course you can reach me. I've been waiting for you." Even if you don't, there are a couple hazards designed to slow your ball and prevent it from rolling into the water. You hope.

Cook's Creek is one of many overnight getaways where the smart players go first to the course and play, then check in to the hotel, and then play the next day before gassing up and heading home. It's one of the many joys of Ohio getaways. You really get away, but you're never far away.

Another joy is the choice of lodging. We stayed in cottages, lodges, state park resorts, hotels, and now—a boutique. Whatever you thought when you saw boutique, forget it. **The Lofts** is a boutique hotel in the middle of Columbus. Whoops. The way Columbus annexes property, the center is probably unknown. But The Lofts is busy enough you'll need to consider rush hour en route to the course. Valet parking helps here.

Big deal. The place is unlike any other and a special treat you owe yourself. The Lofts wasn't built as a hotel. It was built as some sort of factory. We think some sort of harnesses, either horse or electric, were made here. Instead of leveling the place for something new, it was recreated with minimal structural change and the results are handsome. The way Humphrey Bogart was handsome. Even the color scheme is like Bogart: black and white. And shades of gray. Walls are bare brick. Always have been and always will be. The ancient elevator inspires Catholics to mumble the Act of Contrition.

Built in 1882, the structural changes left a mere forty-four rooms, all with high ceilings and windows. It is only five stories and sits hard by the Crown Plaza hotel, like a proud kid introducing his great grandfather. Ancient though it is, the appurtances are thoroughly modern. Can't stand the thought of missing Judge Judy? Two televisions hang from the walls, one in the bedroom and the other in the … uh, other rooms. Another word rarely used in golf travel: concierge. Yup. Staff here is committed to customers and no better example than asking the concierge for directions, advice, or opinion. Ask for directions to North Fourth Street because it also serves as State Route 23, and if you go south, there's Cook's Creek.

None better than these hotel rooms for poker. Management calls the second room a sitting room. We call it heaven. Leather furniture and mini-bar. Here's looking at you, kid.

Man docs not live (long) by booze and birdies alone, and the dining options in the capital city are worthwhile. It's another opportunity to chat with the concierge. We didn't, because right next door, we settled our tired butts into the seats at **Max and Erma's**, a bit of a Columbus legend, and enjoyed very good franchise food.

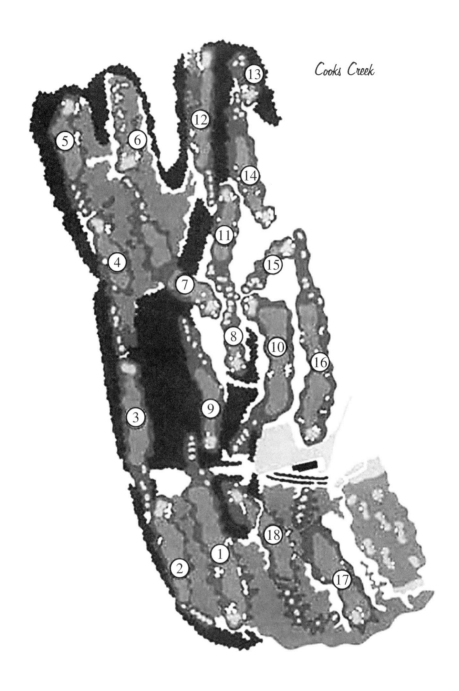

Cooks Creek

STONEWATER GOLF CLUB

1 Club Drive
Highland Heights
440.461.4653
www.stonewatergolf.com

QUAIL HOLLOW COUNTRY CLUB

11295 Quail Hollow Dr.
Concord
440.639.3830

QUAIL HOLLOW RESORT

11080 Concord-Hambden Rd.
Painesville
440.497.1100

Stonewater Golf Club is just like the teenage kid you think will never amount to anything. After being used for a few years between owners like a soccer ball, Stonewater has settled down, grown up, and today presents itself like a member of the State Department.

It was originally to be called Aberdeen, in honor of the Scottish course. When builders found stone enough to quarry just under the surface, quarry they did, and built handsome stone walls on tees, greens, bunkers, and ground water of all sort. The number of stones, set by hand, is well into five figures and makes a very handsome distinction to the track.

While balls occasionally ricochet off the stonework, the stuff wasn't put there for caroms, but for aesthetics. Stone and water are distinguishing characteristics of this course, designed in 1996 by Columbus designers Hurdzan/Fry.

The designers had two of the three features most desired by designers: woods and water. They didn't get elevation, but with 180 acres to work with, they did wonders without it. In addition to the stonework, protected marshlands, more than five dozen sand bunkers (and, oh, what bunkers), and water—some sneaky and some blatant—little wonder the course rating is a frightening 74.8.

Playing from the tips is advised only for low, single-digit players who slept well the night before and had a good, high protein breakfast before arriving.

With five tees, the length can be reduced to just a touch over 5,000 yards and becomes eminently playable.

The practice facilities are terrific; the huge practice green duplicates the speed and undulations to be found on the course and the grass driving range, with target flags, is huge.

By all means, warm up. Don't worry about missing your tee time; the first tee is a bit of a jaunt from the range. The starter will be over in time to call your names and presently, to wish you a good round. He will explain the protected wetlands, the creek and the small lake, the mounding and bunkering, all features of the opening hole.

We didn't say it to management, but we think the best way to play Stonewater is to play No. 1, then come back to the first tee and begin the match, playing it again. No. 1 is a straightaway, with the marshes, a lake, a meandering creek, mounding and bunkers. Hitting into any one of them precludes par on the first hole. The second hole almost says, "Hey, I was kidding, here's a nice, long, wide, straight par 4." At No. 3, the first par 3 is gorgeous, a peninsula green and mostly carry over water with big sand on the other side.

Stone and water are distinguishing characteristics of this course, designed in 1996 by Columbus designers Hurdzan & Fry.

No. 4 is a shot maker's par 5, with the short approach carrying a stonewalled moat. No. 8 is our favorite, maybe because we parred it, but it begins with a tee shot over water, and the fairway runs almost perpendicular to the tee. It's a risk and reward tee shot. Clearing the big, steep-sided sand that protects the fairway is worth at least two clubs for the approach, but hitting either short or long is punishable. Aiming left of the sand makes the approach substantially longer, but safer. That's why they call it risk and reward. In any event, hitting through the fairway is trouble with a capital T and that rhymes with B and that stands for Bogey.

Among the more memorable holes on the back side are No. 10, a short par 4 protected by a minor ravine; No. 13, a par 5 known to cause nightmares in the dreams of strong men; and No. 18, an uphill finishing par 5 that depends far more on shot control than strength.

One caution: The housing here sometimes gets too close to the golf.

Stonewater Golf Club was lagniappe on a trip to **Quail Hollow Resort,** in Painesville, and **Quail Hollow Country Club**, in Concord, which has two wonderful courses; the more recent a Tom Weiskopf layout that drifts and bumps through gorgeous countryside and takes advantage of the elevations on the land. Bruce Devlin and Jay Morrish did the first course, home for a few years to what has evolved into the Nationwide Tour.

The resort and the golf club are separate entities, but getaways are available, and the lobster mashed potatoes in CK's, the resort restaurant, take comfort food to a new culinary level. If we didn't fear embarrassing ourselves, we would have asked the chef to serve us a triple order of his spuds and nothing else. Yes, they are that good.

For players who have not been to the club in recent years, a beautiful surprise awaits. The club built its own clubhouse and it's quite a ways from the old pro shop.

We walked back to the hotel to ask about the missing pro shop. Turns out the club members wanted better than sharing the space with hotel guests, so they anteed up millions and built their own clubhouse. Beautiful it is. Should be; they had to raise $8 million to build the 20,000 square feet facility.

> Remember, Quail is a country club and the resort is a resort. The club is in Concord and the resort is in Painesville. Their relationship is only symbiotic.

The club is chock full of members, a rarity these days, but easy to understand given three factors: the new clubhouse, the two great courses and the hardest working head pro in town, Olle Karlstrom. Not only does he keep these courses in championship condition, he takes care of a very large golf membership, he reports to Club Corp., which owns it, and he's the go-to guy for outings. More than 100 every season. So while an outing has one course, his members have the other.

We have only played here in the autumn and never regretted it. The foliage is knockout and the superintendent makes sure we don't need to institute the leaf rule.

We were given a map at the front desk, and jumped in the car for the brief ride. On the hotel brochure, it brags that the new course is a links course. Nothing could be further from the truth. It is parkland, carved from tall stands of hardwood.

Scorecards are, as they should be, serviceable, but we found something on these scorecards we've never seen before: exclamation marks! Here are a couple examples. "Proper golf attire is mandatory for the course and driving range! No denim!" Our favorite was, "French drains are GUR!" (Don't ask what a French drain is because we have no idea.) And a couple rules without exclamation marks, "… hats worn forward," and this somewhat confusing note, "… keep all four cart wheels on the path." Go figure.

(Here's a tip that might prove valuable: Ask if any leagues are playing on the days you plan to play. On one day, we were shackled to the end of a women's league. Like Donner's Pass, impossible to get through.)

Weiskopf's course is old fashioned and elegant, an up-and-down ride through the woods. Weiskopf has often said his design influences were the great, classic designers, men such as MacKenzie, Ross, Tillinghast, MacDonald and Flynn. Growing up in northeast Ohio, and playing his college golf at Ohio State, Weiskopf played many of their courses.

The designer would be surprised if he played it today. The course has been slightly changed to accommodate the new clubhouse. No change in the holes, just a little crimp in the order. Play begins at what used to be No. 2 and finishes on what used to be No. 1. Without this slight shift, the finishing hole would be far from the clubhouse.

One of the great things about the Weiskopf course is its honesty—no tricks, no surprises. He allows players to see what shots they need for par, and, if they don't have those shots in the bag, alternative routes and strategies are easy to determine. Would that egos were so easily reined in. His use of water and woods is simply wonderful and his skill creating short par 4s pays homage to his ancient design predecessors. Weiskopf reminds us (probably because we keep forgetting), that golf is a thinking man's game.

It is par 71 and from the waybacks it is 6,872 yards, with a slope of 133 and a course rating (ready?) of 74.6.

The Devlin course, created by Bruce Devlin and Jay Morrish, has been host to a number of important qualifiers and PGA tournaments. Signature hole has to be No. 9, a par 4 that begins straightaway. Until it stops. Ah, and then we look way, way, way, downhill. It's a dogleg left and the green is well protected. Not that it needs it, but it is. So players have to hit long enough to get to the edge, but not so long they topple over.

This eighteen, from the tips, plays 6,799 yards, par 72, 133 slope and a course rating of 73.3. But it can be trimmed as short as 4,492, par 72, slope of 121 and course rating of 67.7.

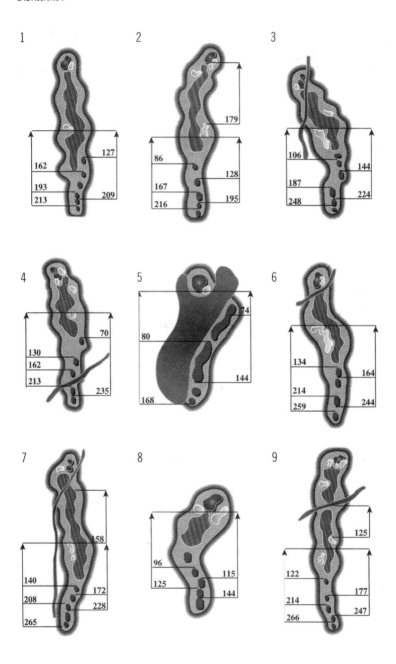

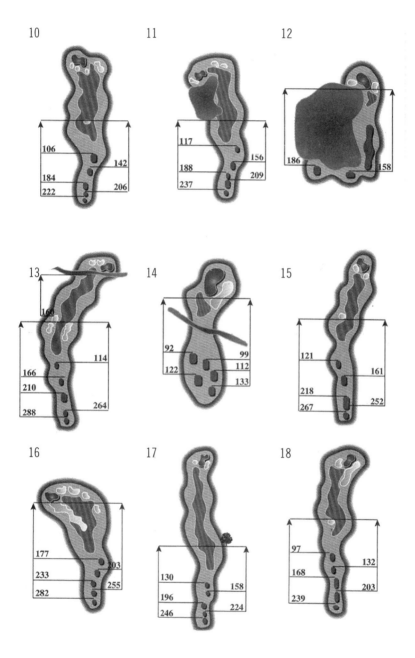

Little Mountain Country Club

7667 Hermitage Rd.
Concord
440.358.7888
www.littlemountaincc.com

Fitzgerald's Irish Bed & Breakfast

47 Mentor Ave.
Painesville
440.639.0845

Brennan's Fish House

102 River St.
Grand River
440.354.9785

Not to tell you how to live your life, but a memorable (read: repeatable) getaway can be had by following these directions: First, play **Little Mountain Country Club**; second, enjoy dinner at **Brennan's Fish House;** third, settle in at **Fitzgerald's Irish Bed and Breakfast**; fourth, return to Little Mountain for another round.

The golf club is in Concord, Brennan's is in Grand River and Fitzgerald's is in Painesville. They are closer to each other than Winken, Blinken and Nod.

Little Mountain, at 1,227 feet above sea level, is not quite a mountain, but a name like Big Hill hardly has the same cachet.

When the design team Hurdzan/Fry first arrived in Concord, it found a designer's dream: Plenty of mature trees, water and lots of changes in elevation. Walking and carrying would be restricted to marathoners with single digit handicaps. Hurdzan/Fry made the most of it.

Golf Digest, after careful consideration, nailed five stars on the front door here. That perfect rating puts Little Mountain at the same table as Bethpage Black, Spyglass Hill, Pinehurst #2, Bandon Dunes, Pebble Beach, Arcadia Bluffs, and Whistling Straits.

Little Mountain opened in 2000, and last year was host to the

Ohio Open.

An unheralded virtue is the first tee. It's a good way to start a game, a straightaway par 5 with a wide fairway and a green jammed into the side of a rise. Tall trees surround the back of the green. But that's not the unheralded virtue. The tee box is a couple hundred yards down the cart path, so when teeing up the first ball of the day, there is no one watching.

Holes No. 2 and 3 are equally playable, the first a brief par 3 with a big, flat green, and then one of the short par 4s that is more deceptive than light cigarets.

No one has been reported missing, but the bunkers can be 20 feet deep.

It is the third elevated tee. Water runs down the left side before circling the base of the elevated green. Only 327 yards from the whites, 366 yards from the blues, and with a wide fairway, most players start sniffing birdie. All it takes is two well-executed shots: the tee shot to the right spot and then a short iron to get on. But woe to the guy who misses either one. If the ball lands in either the left side creek or the water around the green, give up on birdie. Give up on par, too. Rocks around the base of the green will send the ball in myriad directions, none planned on or hoped for.

No. 8 is the other short par 4 and big hitters can't help but go for the green. It is 341 yards from the blues, 302 yards from the whites, and from an elevated tee. While deep sand bunkers protect the left side, a big hit has room to bounce on.

Sand. By this hole, the number and depravity of sand will be apparent. One version of shooting your age on this course is landing in all seventy bunkers. No one has been reported missing, but the bunkers can be twenty feet deep. They are not gimmicks, but forthright demands on the strategic player.

For all the target golf on the front side, the back side calls for muscle as well as brains. If the front side is fascinating, the back side is sheer drama.

Get out the howitzer for Nos. 10 and 11, a brace of gorgeous par 4s with enough risk and reward to attract insurance executives. And finishing holes 17 and 18 are among the best in the state.

From the tee box on No. 17, Lake Erie is in the distance. The only par 5 on the back side, it tumbles downhill only to run into a phalanx of sand bunkers. Feeling lucky? Can you nail a downhill lie to the green? Maybe you can.

The home hole is long and dangerous. Wide open fairway races downhill, then abruptly and steeply pulls up at the huge green. It was on this green, incidentally, that Director of Golf Jimmy Hanlin was married.

Great clubhouse with good food, drink and a pro shop. Even better, Little Mountain's marketing department came up with the Little Mountain Calendar. On the cover are eight, gorgeous women in attire that wouldn't normally be allowed on the course. Inside, the pictures are even better. High heels in the sand and on the green. Each woman in the calendar is an employee or former employee. Calendar is $20, which makes it a far better deal than a ball marker.

Let's eat.

Brennan's Fish House, at the intersection of Lake Erie and Grand River, has a five-page menu. They could easily cut that down to one blackboard and chalk on it, "Perch, Walleye and Crab Cakes."

It's a big, old, two-story, wooden hotel built in the late 1800s when the clientele was mainly sailors and fishermen. On the first floor, they wanted shots and beers and plates filled with good food. Later, they wanted the carnal pleasures available, for a price, upstairs.

Enter the Sullivan Sisters, whose bordello offered love, however transient and ephemeral, for sale. If their ghosts are there, owner Sharon Hill hasn't bumped into them. Good thing. Ms. Hill is still embarrassed (and blushes) about the Sullivans.

One part of the second floor is the office and the other is home to Ms. Hill, her husband and kids. That's one reason it closes at 10 p.m., little later on weekends.

The place was renamed about forty years ago when Tim and Betty Brennan took over. They built its reputation one perch at a time and the restaurant became a favorite of tourists as well as locals.

Ms. Hill, a stay-at-home mom, wondered one day about going to work. What the heck, the kids were older and self-sufficient and she saw an ad in the local paper for a hostess at Brennan's.

Mr. Brennan answered the phone and told her, "Get out of your pajamas and get over here." How he knew she was in her pajamas at 9:30 in the morning speaks to his knowledge of human nature.

She loved the place and the people. When Mr. Brennan announced his plans to sell it and enjoy retirement, Ms. Hill's first thought was to quit. The idea of working for someone besides the Brennans would be untenable.

Her second thought skipped a great many spaces: She wanted to buy it. She did. Somehow, from part-time hostess to owner is a leap seen only in fiction, but she landed on both feet. Nothing has changed at Brennan's. It's big, high-ceilinged, informal.

If the perch were any fresher, they would still be squirming in the net. A walleye fillet is so good it gives pause. And the hand-crafted crab cakes are so rich with crab and delicately flavored, putting cocktail sauce on them is a sin. A venial sin, but still. An aside: the greasy French fries here are the stuff of legend.

And a place to rest your weary head. **Fitzgerald's Irish Bed & Breakfast,** in the heart of Painesville, is a Tudor mansion with slate roof, Historic Register designation, woodwork (including floors) more handsome than Fabio and, in deference to the Irish love of books, wing chairs and reading lamps throughout.

This is Lace Curtain Irish available to the hoi-polloi. A big dining room with an equally big dining room table, lighted by a huge and hypnotic crystal chandelier. A fireplace room with another crystal chandelier, a room so rich and warm you'll want to stay up late to finish your book. The only thing missing is the faint smell of burning peat.

Upstairs is equally elegant. Room names are Galway, Dublin, Bushmill and Mayo. For all the classic design and furniture, the technological amenities are here, too, though latching on to Wi-fi somehow breaks the mood.

Hot breakfast on weekends include French toast stuffed with whatever freshest fruit can be found at the market, homemade scones just as good as your great-grandmother's, an indulgent egg dish in a potato pie crust.

The innkeepers, Debra and Tom Fitzgerald, also have full time careers outside Fitzgerald's, and prepare a continental breakfast during the week. It includes the usual, plus fresh-sliced fruits and whatever breakfast breads Tom baked the night before.

The dining room table is wonderful for poker and gin, but it's the backyard that might be perfect. Poker al fresco, as it were. The huge backyard is a manicured garden with a high wooden fence, towering oak tree, ivy border, bubbling fountain, red brick pathways and ashtrays. Either shuffle the deck while there is still light or plan on playing under a full moon.

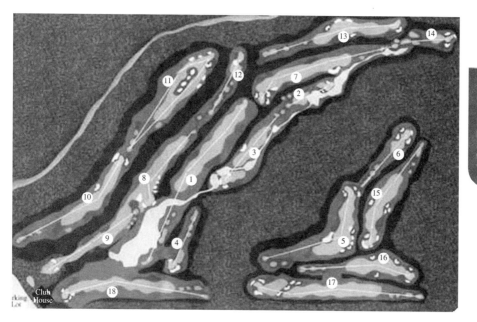

PUNDERSON STATE PARK

11755 Kinsman Rd.

Newbury

800.282.7275

Pro shop 440.564.5465

www.pundersonmanorstateparklodge.com

Number 8. That's the one. That's the one that separates the men from the boys, the wheat from the chaff, the sweet corn from the feed corn.

For guys playing **Punderson State Park** the first time, No. 8 is an ambush for the unwary. It is where the wild things are.

We asked the pro if we could just skip the hole and pencil in a 7. No deal, he said. We then suggested crying towels be offered at the back of the green. This is golf, not grief therapy, he said. The holes here are numbered and not named. We suggested to the pro that No. 8, in addition to its number, have a name and we wanted to call it Purgatory. Forget about it, he said.

Not to say it's a chamber of horrors; it's a gorgeous hole, with woods and water and up and down. Neither is it long, only 411 yards from the white tees. And that is mostly downhill, after all. On the other hand, it's the number one handicap for good reason. This is not the tee for launching your power slice or snap hook. When the bottom is reached, it's a bit of a dogleg right over water. It isn't unfair; but it is penal. It calls for an accurate tee shot and then an approach with water staring at you. Aquaphobes rarely par here. It didn't help when one of us gave an off-key rendition of Marty Robbins singing, "Cool Water."

It's the tee shot that gets most of us in trouble, unfamiliar as we are with second shots that demand successfully executing downhill, sidehill shots. Regardless of political affiliation, this is a hole where middle and high handicappers should flaunt their conservatism. The best our foursome did was a bogey, which felt like a birdie.

But back to the opening hole. Old-fashioned, the tee boxes are, with red, white and blue markers. From the back tees, it's almost 6,800 yards, par 72, course rating 72.3 and slope of 125. An excellent and beautiful challenge for single-digit players. Nothing wrong with the whites or reds, either: Whites play 6,600 yards, course rating is 71.2 and slope is 122. The reds, with a 72.3 rating and slope of 122, play 5,200 yards or so.

It's not an old course, built in 1969 and designed by Jack Kidwell. He scattered almost forty bunkers around the course, and there is water enough to pack an extra sleeve. There is no driving range here, a surprise given the amount of land, but the practice green gives a very good indication of green speed on the course. The clubhouse isn't anything to write home about, but who cares—it's not as if we hang around clubhouses after a round.

First couple holes are good holes, especially because they serve as warm up holes. Not to worry—plenty of challenge as the course goes on. Love these greens; they are often big and probably run about 9.0, but they are more true than your high school sweetheart. And unlike her, very, very accommodating. If you can see the line, you can sink the putt.

No. 6 is one of these challenging holes we know we'll play better in the future because now we know what it looks like. It's a 550-yard par 5, but the first two shots, unless you're a gorilla, are blind. The dogleg right is also the first hole with water. There are four lakes here, and they share hazard duty with seven holes: Nos. 6, 8, 9, 11, 12, 14 and 18.

There are thirty-one rooms in the lodge and twenty-six cottages. We took a cottage, the better to "shut up and deal," and could not have been more pleased. Two bedrooms, fully equipped kitchen, and best of all, screened in porch. The cottages sleep six players, but not unless they're closely related. Four works better, separating the snorers and sleepwalkers from those who sleep the sleep of the innocent, for their hearts are pure.

But the lodge is worth a long and leisurely visit. Not just for the restaurant, but to enjoy this old, stone, handsome facility. It is the Punderson Manor, and suddenly, the reality of being "to the manor borne" makes sense. Was there, long ago, a horse drawn carriage in front? Did the lord of the manor step in and tell the driver, "To town, James"?

A brief aside for history: the place is named for Lemuel Punderson, a man with money who started building the English Tudor manor in the late '20s. He also had the audacity to name the lake after himself. It's a pretty good fishin' hole if you're of mind; sixty feet deep in parts, and home to bluegill, largemouth bass, rainbow and golden trout and catfish. Don't get caught without a license.

The manor was built by craftsmen and artisans with detail we'll never see in a modern structure. First-rate stone and lumber. Stonemasons, glaziers, and carpenters laid the foundation and today management treats the lodge like the royal jewel it is. Indoors, even the loudest among us spoke softly. Afraid of waking a ghost? They are already awake. At the front desk, grab the eight-page booklet on ghost sightings. At night, don't look under the bed.

The rooms at the lodge are very nice (windows are leaded glass and they open), but if it's a golf outing and there's a cottage available, cottage trumps. Why wouldn't it? When we play Texas Hold 'Em, our language sometimes tends to the coarse. Plus, with a screened-in back porch on the cottage, is there a better place to trim and fire up a handsome double corona?

The elegance extends to the dining room. The views, it won't surprise you, are idyllic, with the lake on the other side of the windows and ducks and geese clamoring. The restaurant seats 100, and did you know all the employees here are local? We asked about them because every one of the staff seemed personally devoted to us. ('Cept the golf pro, of course.)

We were looking at the dinner menu and then half-expecting Jeeves to arrive and take our drink order. Ved-d-d-y English, it is. Bangers and mash we had, and shepherd's pie, too. One of us, admitting no knowledge of bangers *or* shepherds, went with the sixteen-ounce ribeye. His directions to the guy on the grill were specific: between rare and medium rare. The grill guy nailed it.

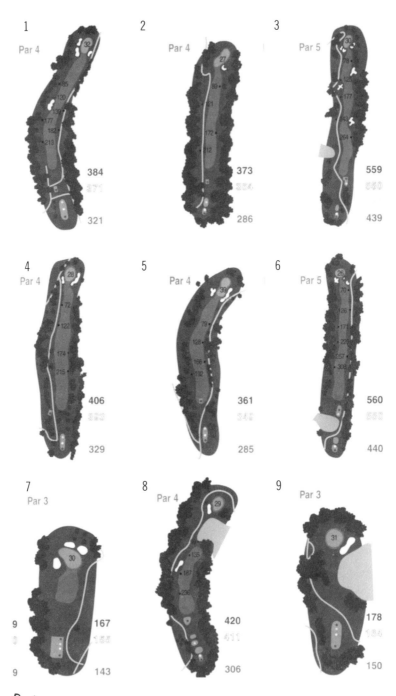

1
Par 4
85
120
139
177
182
213
384
371
321

2
Par 4
27
83
81
72
212
373
354
286

3
Par 5
30
4
125
177
243
264
559
560
439

4
Par 4
28
72
122
174
215
406
329

5
Par 4
38
79
128
166
192
361
285

6
Par 5
25
70
126
171
220
257
308
560
440

7
Par 3
30
9
167
9
143

8
Par 4
29
133
187
236
420
411
306

9
Par 3
31
178
150

Punderson

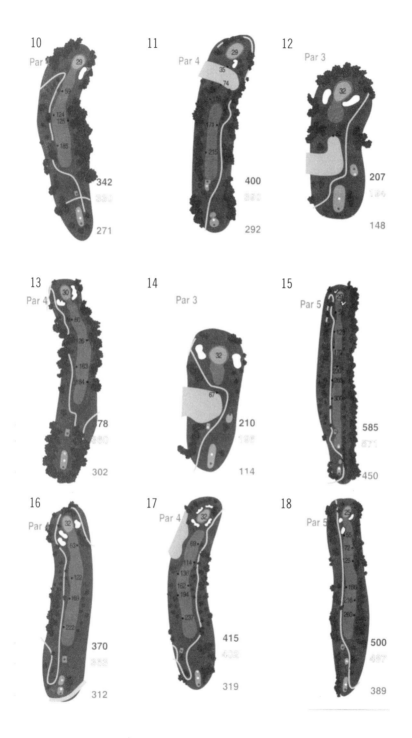

10 Par 4
29
59
124
125
185
342
381
271

11 Par 4
29
35
74
171
215
400
361
292

12 Par 3
32
207
126
148

13 Par 4
30
86
126
163
184
378
360
302

14 Par 3
32
67
210
185
114

15 Par 5
29
129
171
230
255
300
585
671
450

16 Par 4
32
53
122
169
222
370
353
312

17 Par 4
32
68
114
130
162
194
237
415
435
319

18 Par 5
25
55
72
125
180
216
260
500
487
389

CHARDON LAKES GOLF CLUB

470 South St.
Chardon
440.285.4653
www.chardonlakes.com

FOWLER'S MILL GOLF COURSE

13095 Rockhaven Rd.
Chesterland
440.729.7569
www.fowlersmillgc.com

BASS LAKE TAVERN & INN

426 South St.
Chardon
440.285.3100

The really good players at **Fowler's Mill Golf Course** don't think No. 4 is the most challenging hole on the course. The rest of us silently disagree. The dominating feature is water, all fifty-eight acres of it, down the right side and all the way to the elevated green. We walked back to the tips, a peninsula tee, to see what it looked like and we became dizzy. It's 435 yards to the green and legend is that one player drove the green. As your Aunt Louise used to say, "If it's between fact and legend, always go with legend. Makes a better story."

Even from the whites, the water on the right takes in golf balls the way Father Damian used to take in lepers: No questions asked. No returns, either.

Well, what could we expect; it's a Pete Dye course, and, yes, the railroad tie business is better for having him. It wasn't always Fowler's Mill, which is one of the great course names. It started life as a corporate course for TRW, Inc., a Cleveland company with a great engineering history. It still has a presence, but not much. A shame it wasn't able to stay; happy the course was bequeathed to us.

The trip begins with pulling in to the largest parking lot we've ever parked in. There's a bag drop, of course, and on the rise is a new, low-slung, and big clubhouse. Very good grill room, and full service pro shop. When it was built a few years ago, one of the rooms was named for Dye and he attended the dedication ceremony. Based on descriptions from eyewitnesses, he does not have horns. We're surprised (and grateful) he didn't build a redan here. He's been known to, you know.

The course belongs to the Audubon Cooperative Sanctuary Program for Golf Courses. Know what that means, don't you? If the argument is between us and a cedar waxwing, the songbird wins.

Nice grass practice range (irons only) and if you want to know the speed of greens on the course, the practice green matches perfectly. Here's an example of the care taken: A few years ago, management studied the rough (the rough!) and decided it was time to better manicure it. A project to manicure the rough was started and finished.

Fowler's Mill has impressive stands of hardwoods, which allows the course to be insulated with Mother Nature's most impressive stuff. And it's a generous course. At no time did we think Uncle Pete was running out of terrain or had to stick a tee or green where it didn't really belong. There are twenty-seven holes and River and Lake nines make up the primary course; across the road is the runt of the triplets, Maple, which is the best nine-hole warm up track in the history of Ohio golf. It plays about 3,000 yards and offers all sorts of challenge.

The first three holes on the main course, leading up to the legendary No. 4, look easy but are not exactly warm up holes (see Maple nine above), though No. 1, a gentle dogleg left, has a huge landing area. Even so, landing on the wrong side of the fairway means an especially difficult iron to land on the small green. And No. 2 rolls, up and down, with fairway sand, like a kiddie roller coaster, to an elevated green. No. 3 is a difficult and long par 3, made more difficult by the psychological spectre rising from the lake on No. 4. The green on No. 3, not to give it short shrift, is picture perfect thanks to a large tree and equally large bunker. The hole is very well defined.

The lake can be problematic because it is in play for the tee shot and approach. Allowing ourselves to be threatened by the lake, we played middle left, which meant adding yardage to the hole. This is one of those holes played better by blind golfers.

Walking off the No. 4 green, through a glade to the fifth tee reminded us: 1.) This really is a Pete Dye course and 2.) Nothing wrong with bogey golf. Once we all agreed, playing this magnificent course is pure delight. It pitches and rolls, caroms and twists, turns without warning and is a constant pleasure for the eye. Fall foliage is nothing if it isn't breathtaking.

No. 9 isn't long, but a fairway split with a creek offers a shorter and riskier path to the green. Republicans go right, Democrats go left. Their scores even out, but listening to Republicans curse the Great Goddess of Golf adds a dollop of entertainment.

The grill room really is good, but this is no time for a beer and chips; an energy bar and quart of Gatorade is the meal of choice.

Nos. 12 and 13, in our opinion, constitute the best consecutive par 4 and par 3 on the course (and on any number of courses). Twelve is (yet another) split fairway. We didn't think landing in either fairway provided a great reward, but joining the GOP and going right was prudent. And then that par 3. Ah, yes, that par 3. Few par 3s are intimidating. This one is. When they say uphill, they don't mean gently rising. Oh, no. Fairway is flat and then the green takes off like a missile launched from an underground silo. The tree on the left edge of the green has enough board feet it in to build a rain shelter. So club selection is more important, at this point, than paying your cell phone bill. Anything not on the green pretty much guarantees square(s) around the scores. Who can pitch accurately from a steep, uphill lie in the rough? If ever there was a call for a toe mashie, this is it.

The home hole is a big, beautiful par 5 and as long as we stayed in the fairway, we did well. All in all, one of Ohio's great tracks. It's big, lush, good-looking, staffed with friendly professionals, and again—it's a Pete Dye course. Pete Dye, the diabolical, dastardly, devious, dangerous, delightful, demanding, dynamic, daring—the guy is a golf treasure.

Just down the street from the Inn is **Chardon Lakes Golf Club**. Know what the course record is? Sixty-seven. Know who holds it? Jack Nicklaus. Know who designed it? Here are a couple hints: the guy also created the lumbering behemoth, Firestone South, and he was second in the 1899 U.S. Open. Ladies and gentlemen, pre-e-e-e-e-sen-ting the late, great Bertie Way. Next year the course will be 80 years old. You should live so long.

That reminds us that with the proper care and feeding, good courses outlive their designers. (See: Edsel Ford.)

The course is neither extra long nor treacherous, which made us wonder why Nicklaus could only shoot a 67. (Sorry, did we say *only* a 67?) Once around this very pretty course, we figured it out: If you can't stay in the short grass, can't putt, don't have recovery shots in your bag, are allergic to pine trees, don't play by the rules (never once did Nicklaus tell a playing partner on the first tee, "Oh, go ahead. Hit 'til you're happy"), or any combination, the course is strict. That and the fact that none of us plays from the tips. Strict, this course is, but not penal. Neither clubhouse nor golf course overwhelm; instead, both impress and invite. Not only is the staff here proud of the course, the customers are, too. For many, a week without eighteen holes here is just not a good week.

The Inn is a big, white frame, a good-looking century home that works well in this century, too. We wonder what the original owner would think if he walked into one of the bathrooms and saw the jacuzzi whizzing and gurgling.

Bass Lake Tavern & Inn has a getaway package with Chardon Lakes, but passing up a chance to also play Fowler's Mill, which is just around the corner, would insult the Royal and Ancient. That you don't want to do.

Dress for dinner here. You know the place is good because so many area residents make it a regular stop. And be seated with high hopes; this might be one of the best dinners on the getaway tour: mussels and crab cakes, lake perch with remoulade sauce, and rabbit paprikash, among other offerings. Now, just a note about the remoulade sauce: it's a Cajun sauce that is good smeared on seafood, but if you don't have seafood, dipping your fingers in it is just as good. Now, just a note about rabbit paprikash. At home, we've made venison paprikash, also veal and chicken. Like the remoulade, if you have any sauce left over, it's worth dipping a couple fingers.

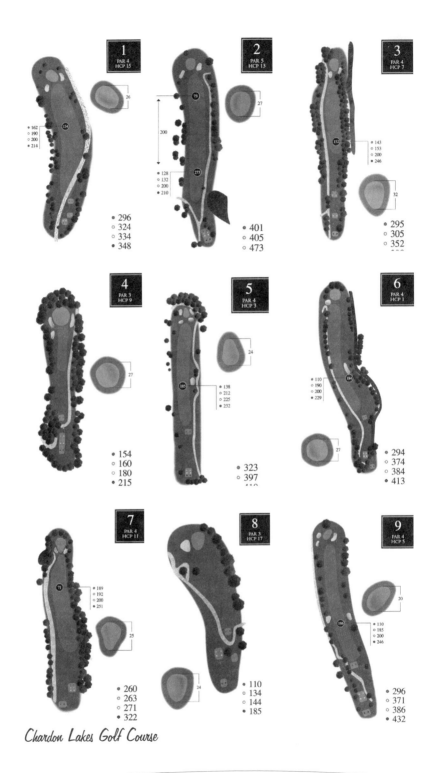

1 PAR 4 HCP 15

26

- 162
- 190
- 200
- 214

134

- 296
- 324
- 334
- 348

2 PAR 5 HCP 13

27

73

200

- 128
- 132
- 200
- 210

273

- 401
- 405
- 473

3 PAR 4 HCP 7

152

- 143
- 153
- 200
- 246

32

- 295
- 305
- 352

4 PAR 3 HCP 9

27

- 154
- 160
- 180
- 215

5 PAR 4 HCP 3

24

185

- 138
- 212
- 225
- 232

- 323
- 397

6 PAR 4 HCP 1

- 110
- 190
- 200
- 229

184

27

- 294
- 374
- 384
- 413

7 PAR 4 HCP 11

71

- 189
- 192
- 200
- 251

25

- 260
- 263
- 271
- 322

8 PAR 3 HCP 17

24

- 110
- 134
- 144
- 185

9 PAR 4 HCP 5

20

186

- 110
- 185
- 200
- 246

- 296
- 371
- 386
- 432

Chardon Lakes Golf Course

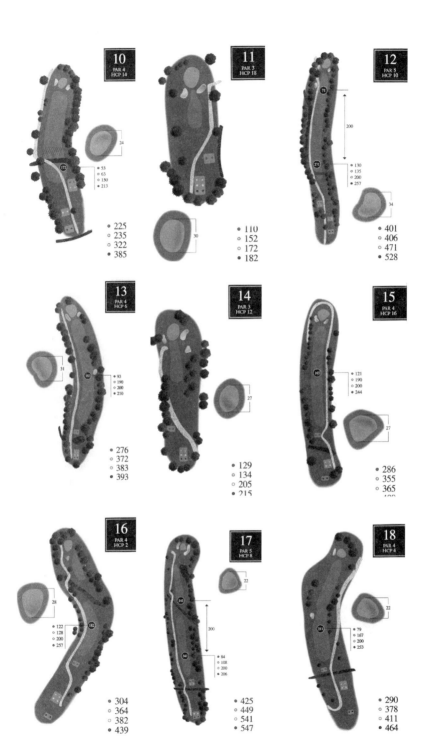

10
PAR 4
HCP 14

• 53
○ 63
□ 130
• 213

24

172

• 225
○ 235
□ 322
• 385

11
PAR 3
HCP 18

30

• 110
○ 152
□ 172
• 182

12
PAR 5
HCP 10

71

200

271

• 130
○ 135
□ 200
• 257

34

• 401
○ 406
□ 471
• 528

13
PAR 4
HCP 6

31

183

• 93
○ 190
□ 200
• 210

• 276
○ 372
□ 383
• 393

14
PAR 3
HCP 12

27

• 129
○ 134
□ 205
• 215

15
PAR 4
HCP 16

165

• 121
○ 190
□ 200
• 244

27

• 286
○ 355
□ 365

16
PAR 4
HCP 2

28

182

• 122
○ 128
□ 200
• 257

• 304
○ 364
□ 382
• 439

17
PAR 5
HCP 8

22

141

200

141

• 84
○ 108
□ 200
• 206

• 425
○ 449
□ 541
• 547

18
PAR 4
HCP 4

22

211

• 79
○ 167
□ 200
• 253

• 290
○ 378
□ 411
• 464

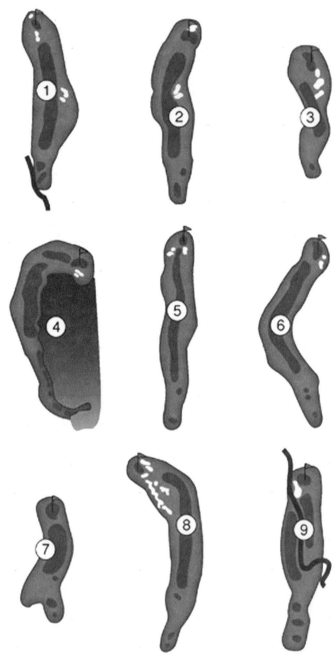

Fowler's Mill

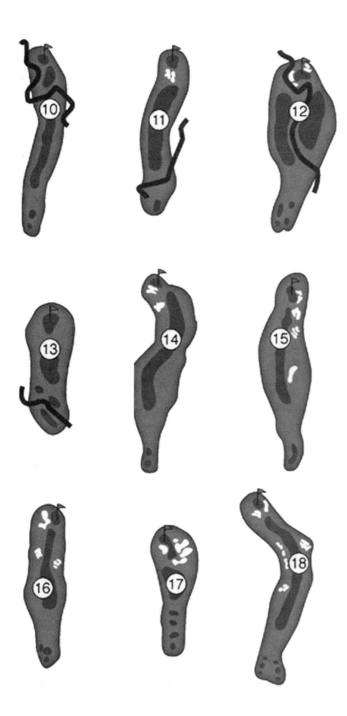

SLEEPY HOLLOW GOLF COURSE

9445 Brecksville Rd.
Cleveland
440.526.4285
www.clemetparks.com

MARRIOTT RESIDENCE INN

527 Prospect Ave.
Cleveland
216.443.9043

MANAKIKI GOLF COURSE

35501 Eddy Rd.
Willoughby Hills
440.942.2500
www.clemetparks.com

Long before hotel chains realized there was money to be made by arranging golf getaways, there was The Guy in every group who did all the work: making hotel reservations, getting tee times, letting everyone know where they were going and how to get there.

What follows is a homemade getaway so good and so memorable, the slackers will happily buy dinner for The Guy, even though that dinner won't come cheap.

Welcome to Cleveland, famous for some major accomplishments (the 1948 Indians and 1964 Browns are recent examples) and infamous for others (Sam Sheppard, John Demjanjuk, and Louie the Dip, a pickpocket so inept he had a nickname), but never known as a golf getaway. Three of the elements in this one, lodging and two tremendous courses, are historic, and dinners are the sort that keep cardiologists in business.

Not to be boringly tangential, but the history parts of this getaway will provide sweet memories and vows to return. **Sleepy Hollow Golf Course** is one of seven courses owned and managed by Cleveland Metroparks. It was here that black golf pro Charlie "Little Horse" Sifford held court as club pro. (If you want to read a shocking story about the PGA and its "whites only" clause, Sifford's biography, *Just Let Me Play,* is just the ticket.)

In a dozen or so years, Sleepy Hollow will celebrate its centennial. Course designer Stanley Thompson's name and visage will be dragged out of the storage locker and properly acknowledged. While Thompson would recognize instantly his powerful course, the clubhouse would surprise him. The old clubhouse was laid to waste a few years ago and on its site was built a big, functional, comfortable clubhouse more in keeping with Sleepy Hollow's pre-eminence in northern Ohio golf. Positives: lots of windows overlook the 10th tee; rear deck provides views of No. 1; big grill room; television is usually on the Golf Channel; showers and phone in locker rooms; big rooms for end-of-league-season parties. Negatives: tee times can be reserved only one week ahead; kitchen is small and menu isn't keeping with the rest of the place; pro shop is too tightly packed.

A ravine runs down the right side, trees overhang on the left. This is not your muni course par 3.

Thompson, that brilliant designer from long ago and far away, built a gem in 1925. It was a private club from the dedication round until 1963, when it became public. Someone noticed that Sleepy Hollow, a private club, was on public park land and sued. No sense subsidizing rich people. Goodbye membership committee and hello trunk slammers. The parks system made sure Sleepy Hollow wouldn't fall back to puny course standards; it remains in country club condition.

Sleepy Hollow is an every-stick-in-the-bag course and to score well, players have to bring the A game: Long off the tee, accurate with irons, great short game. Fast, swerving greens, troublesome rough, great changes in elevation, couple great short par 4s, powerful par 5s, and the course is surrounded by woods. No homes, no development.

Tee times are ten minutes apart, which allows play to constantly move. The game begins with a straightaway, downhill par 5, but the course quickly bares its fangs on Nos. 2 and 3. No. 2 usually plays around 225 yards.

Only the best players get on No. 2 with an iron; the rest flail away with fairway woods or drivers. The direction given by the tee box is a fooler; it's more to the right than it appears. The wise mid- or high-handicapper lays up, pitches on to the two-level green and leaves relieved with a bogey, ecstatic with a par. A ravine runs down the right side, trees overhang on the left. This is not your muni course par 3.

And that begins the front nine, where big hitters are welcome and the weak among us are humbled yet again. But the back is different. The back nine at Sleepy Hollow may be the best back nine this side of the Mississippi. It begins with another long hole, a par 4, but there are no hidden hazards. Then the great roller coaster ride begins. Over hill and dale, around stands of hardwoods, over water and ravine, and on to small greens, a reflection of the era in which they were built. No. 13 is a good example. The tee box is in a valley and the tee shot is blind. Once up and out, players look over a deep ravine to a narrow fairway heading due right. For the second shot, you still can't see the flag, but with the right stick and the right swing, setting up is eminently doable and leaves only a short approach to a flat green. It is followed by a short par 4 with the toughest green on the course. Distance on the tee shot has to be limited and controlled, and the approach, over a steep valley to a green that falls precipitously on three sides, should land beneath the hole if there is to be a reasonable chance of par. Putting downhill on this fast green means your next shot will be with a wedge.

The practice range is mats, which is a venial sin; the practice green is one of the best.

'Nuff said about Sleepy Hollow? Wait till you hear about the other bookend on this getaway: Manakiki. But first things first.

It would be difficult to say enough about the **Marriott Residence Inn,** in downtown Cleveland. For purposes of golf getaways, that is. Almost as if the Great God of Golf created the place, taking into account groups' needs for room, comfort and pocket billiards.

The place is by East Fourth Street, today jammed with so many restaurants and bars that they have spilled into the street and cars are no longer welcome. The House of Blues is there, *Iron Chef* winner Michael Symon has a place, and on the other corner a new and fun bowling alley. Bob Dylan made the street famous when he wrote and sang, "Positively Fourth Street."

The hotel is 120 years old and started life as the Colonial Hotel. A decade or so ago, Marriott found value in the old hotel and went about updating, refurbishing, rewiring, renovating and tearing out walls. A few important virtues remain. The hallways are wide and tall, the rooms quiet and comfortable and when the room door closes, that solid oak is impenetrable. Taking a full swing in the rooms with an eight-iron is not likely to damage the crown molding.

(Editor's Note: That line about Bob Dylan and downtown Cleveland was a complete fabrication.)

One hundred twenty years ago, travelers didn't expect large rooms. Or kitchens. When the renovators arrived, they knocked down walls to make two-bedroom suites and in the middle is a kitchen with full size refrigerator, stove, disposal, coffee maker, dishwasher and cupboards. Inside the cupboards and drawers guests find dinnerware, kitchen utensils, cups, glasses and flatware. Every bed is a king.

The Colonial must have been big; when the dust cleared, Marriott was still left with 175 rooms. The hotel is part of an arcade, an architectural delight that connects, in this case, Prospect and Euclid avenues. Arches rise and meet at the top. Offices, shops and stores are on each level.

Breakfast is served in a beautiful, big, formal dining room. Stained glass windows, created more than a century ago, grace the top of the wall. Poker, acey-deucey, blackjack, and gin can be enjoyed there, and it's open all night. Just off the lobby is a warm, woody, billiards parlor with two tables.

Now, how to connect the hotel to the first golf course. Easy and sort of fun. I-77 is just a couple blocks from the hotel. Jump on and head south. Traffic is very light. Traffic coming the other direction, the poor fools trying to get to the office on time, is very, very heavy. This is the perfect opportunity to roll down the windows and yell at the proletariat, "Sweat on, taxpayers!" One turn off the interstate and one more turn to Brecksville Road and Sleepy Hollow. Same traffic pattern coming back.

Shower and dress for dinner, which is just a couple blocks from the hotel. Morton's, the steakhouse, from the street looks like just another new office building. Inside, it is another world—the welcome is warm, lighting is subdued, the maître d wears a perfectly pressed tuxedo.

Now going to your table is the usual, but we opted for Bar 12.21, the long and woody barroom off to the right. The numbers in the name, by the way, mark the opening of the first Morton's, in Chicago, on December 21, more than thirty years ago. Provenance and pedigree.

Couple great features: generous drinks and killer appetizers. Even better, the full dinner menu is available in the bar. Ah, that menu. We were there for beef, but there is also fresh fish and lobsters, sea scallops and smoked salmon.

But the beef. Not often do we get a chance to enjoy prime aged beef. What's your pleasure? A double cut filet? A ribeye? A magnificent porterhouse? Lamb chops?

We left sated, after one perfect martini, a dozen bluepoints on the half shell and a ribeye to die for.

The guys who stay up late will regret it playing **Manakiki Golf Course** the next morning. Getting there is a ride into the rising sun, but again, all the traffic is going the other way. Interstate 90, coupla turns, there's the bag drop.

This is a classic Donald Ross design and one the ol' Scotsman loved. Great piece of parkland property, lots of changes in elevation, some water, but not a lot.

Ross loved good iron play to small greens. Eminently fair, big landing areas, minimal bunkering. Lots of beautiful ups and downs. With innovative maintenance, lots of holes are dramatic; they give pause. Front side is just a little hilly, back side is very hilly. Maintenance here is first rate and efforts to maintain the original design are laudatory as well as beautiful.

No. 1 gives no hint of the round at hand. It's a blind tee shot with little visual direction. When this was pointed out to one of the golf professionals there, he thought for a moment and said, "Yeah … but it's Manakiki." Nos. 2 and 3 suddenly show off the course and the design. Every hole is different, and selecting a signature hole proves difficult. But if you can find a more beautiful, challenging finishing hole, you must be playing in a parallel universe.

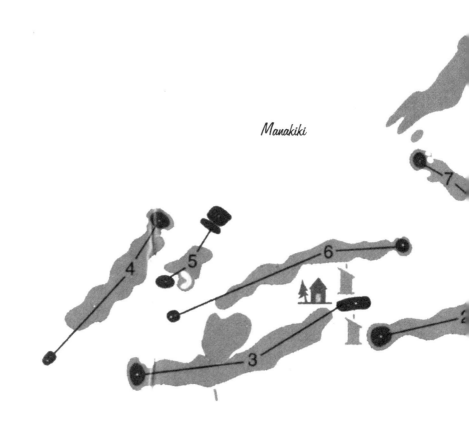

Manakiki

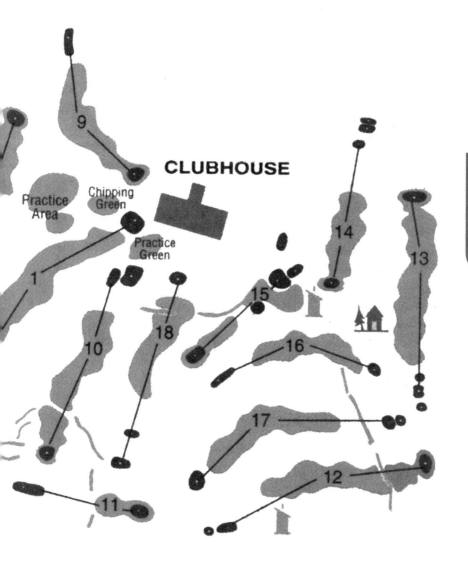

CLUBHOUSE

Practice Area

Chipping Green

Practice Green

9

1

10

18

15

16

17

11

12

14

13

EMERGENCIES

As the Boy Scouts remind us, "Be Prepared." Here are a number of common emergencies and how to deal with them. When we say, "how to deal with them," what we mean is how to deal with them so they don't upset the getaway.

Here's the best example. At Skyland GC, a foursome was on the third tee. These guys played regularly and always had a few bucks on the game. Suddenly, one of the players grabbed his chest and announced he was having a heart attack. The other three guys were rightly skeptical. The malingerer wasn't playing well; was he trying to get out of the bet?

When he insisted he really was having The Big One, the rest of the foursome put their heads together and quickly came up with a solution. Because they didn't believe the complainer, they took him over to the nearby seventh green and promised that after they played Nos. 3,4,5,6, and 7, they would inquire again. If his story remained the same, they would take him to the clubhouse.

That's just what they did. They took him to the seventh green and hurried back to the tee. The No. 3 hole, by the way, is gorgeous. A short par 5 of 512 yards, but it's from an elevated tee. The landing area on the tree-lined fairway is generous. The fairway bottoms out about halfway to the cup, then rises to the green. It's reachable, though hitting uphill and stopping the ball on the green is not easy. On the left side of the fairway, a hundred yards from the green, is a towering American Elm. Don't see those very often.

Anyway, the now-threesome teed off and played. A golfer coming up to the seventh green noticed an unusual hazard: some guy lying next to his clubs. "What's the matter with you?" he asked. "I'm having a heart attack." The kindly player raced the patient back to the clubhouse, thereby saving his life. The lesson? When Real Men want to play, they play.

Here are other emergencies and how to deal with them.

Getting lost in the woods.

How to Deal: Hey, it happens. For example, mistaking a hiking trail for the path to the next tee is not uncommon.

Sit down. Curse yourself for not charging your cell phone. Sooner or later, some tree huggers will be strolling by. Latch on.

No clean underwear.

How to Deal: You call that an emergency?

Stomach ache.

How to Deal: Oh, man up, will ya? You're the guy who wouldn't share his slab of baby back ribs last night, so quit yer bitchin'.

A fatal heart attack.

How to Deal: Hey, you were the guy who said he wanted to die on a golf course. Not an emergency as much as it is a wish come true.

Cleaned out at last night's poker game.

How to Deal: Not to worry; you just guaranteed an invitation to the next getaway.

Snorer in the cabin.

How to Deal: There are a number of ways to stop a man from snoring, and many of them, while hazardous, are pretty funny. First, get out the video camera.

THUNDER HILL GOLF CLUB

7050 Griswold Rd.
Madison
440.298.3474
www.thunderhillgolf.com

FERRANTE WINERY & RISTORANTE

5585 State Route 307
Geneva
440.466.8466
www.ferrantewinery.com

It is the course of myth and mystery, a course of swaggering, unapologetic reputation. Merciless and demanding. A machete is a good fourteenth club and there are more fish-filled lakes than there are sand traps. A course rating of 78.5 and a slope of 152.

Thunder Hill Golf Club, in Madison.

When it was designed and built by the late Fred Slagle, all of that was true. Slagle was on a bulldozer, building his course, when a bolt of lighting damn near hit him. The crack of thunder, enough to send shock waves through forest animals, followed immediately. And that is how the course got its name.

The design is more fascinating. Slagle was not a golf course designer; he made his money—lots of it—in commercial real estate.

So he connected with the ephemeral thoughts of golf course designers and using that information, designed and built his own course. A wonderful course he built in 1976, a trip up and down steep hills, in and out of forests, around and over lakes.

Slagle's rough draft was riotous, but not particularly playable. A lack of professional maintenance gave it a shabby texture and a wayward shot into the undergrowth meant a lost ball.

That was then. This is now.

Slagle turned it over to a management company that cleaned things up and a couple years ago, the course was purchased by General Manager Kevin Leymaster and Director of Golf Todd Bishop.

What this team hath wrought.

Leymaster considers Slagle a genius whose strengths did not include marketing or maintenance. But the place had great bones and great potential.

A machete is a good fourteenth club and there are more fish-filled lakes than there are sand traps.

Thunder Hill is a work in progress and likely will always be. But the improvements, changes and services have made the course eminently playable. We think it's more a matter of burnishing its reputation than changing it. With five tees, it is playable and beautiful for high handicappers, and the greatest challenge for single-digits.

They started with creating a top-notch grounds crew: Only six members on the team, which makes it the best organized and hardest working maintenance staff in the history of golf. Then they went about rebuilding a half dozen greens, renovating seventy-nine bunkers, filling in some of the unnecessary lakes and ponds, renovating and changing the focus of the restaurant, marketing the course at golf shows, and rebuilding the lake house to handle groups of a dozen.

This masterpiece begins with a par 4, flanked on both sides by water, bunkered at the green, and shaded by trees. With all the water here, weeping willows stand out among the trees.

The course heads uphill and that's where the course really shows off. Slagle had 220 acres to work with and he used them all.

With all the underbrush gone, the greens and fairways manicured, the physical beauty of the course is the subject of many tee box conversations. Finally, seeing other holes is one of the unnoticed delights.

The four par 3s on the course are memorable. No. 3 can play from 135 yards to 207 yards to a peninsula green. No. 9 plays 200 yards to 250 yards and there's water in the front, but it's a bluff. No. 11 is 125 yards to 175 yards. Thinking birdie here? Think again. This is Thunder's most severe green. Par is wonderful, bogey is worthy, too. No. 16 is the signature par 3 hole here, playing from 125 yards to 145 yards to an enormous green. And behind the green is the lake house, the two-story lodge that had been Slagle's home.

As challenging as it is, the design gives clear direction and hitting a straight ball is a virtue. Again, Thunder Hill can be a joy if only we pick the right tee. For players who think no course is too big for them, the waybacks are 7,504 yards, longer than most PGA Tour stops. The yellow tees are 6,866 yards, the green tees 6,436 yards, the whites 6,003 yards and the blue 4,769 yards.

The lodge, a feature unique to Ohio golf, has five bedrooms and baths, and comfortably fits a dozen, more if they're related. The lodge had been ignored for years, so rehabbing it was neither easy nor inexpensive. It is two stories and four of the five bedrooms open onto the deck that wraps around. On the first floor, there is fishing tackle, so battling a five-pound bass while sipping morning coffee is more interesting than reading the sports page. There's a big, commercial grill on the deck and wall-mounted plasma tellys indoors. The kitchen is fully stocked with pots and pans, dishes of all sizes, cups and glass, forks and spoons. Poker? Somebody say poker? Not only is there a poker room here, but management is having ceramic chips made that will feature Thunder Hill's logo.

Last year the course held a fishing-cum-golf tournament. The guy who won the fish part of it, with a five-pound, twelve -ounce bass (27"), caught the largemouth with a single cast. The golf was 6-6-6: best ball, captain's choice and scramble. Management threw in a great house rule: birdie a hole and you move back a tee; bogey a hole and you move forward a tee. All the tees are in play.

For an outing using the lake house, gear is brought to the house and cars are returned to the parking lot. Guests use carts while they're there.

Just up the road and five miles east is **Ferrante Winery & Ristorante**, an award-winning winery with a knockout dining room. The original place was built by Pete Ferrante, a carpenter. He bought the property in 1937 and after finishing his work, came to the property to create his vineyard and restaurant.

Pete died last year. He was 87 and in very good health until the end. He thought his good health was a matter of enjoying two glasses of wine every day.

The place was torched in 1994 by an arsonist and only the wine-making area was saved. When the family went about rebuilding, they asked the architect to keep in mind Campobasso, the southern Italian province that gave us the Ferrantes.

All the sauces are made on site, using recipes that came with the grandparents from the old country. We started off with a platter overflowing with mussels. Steamed in their chardonnay and served with fresh bread. We ordered steaks, though it's not what Ferrante's is known for. A couple of twelve ounce strips, one rare and one between rare and medium rare. Ordering wine is especially nice. For these plates of beef, either the River Valley cabernet franc, or the pinot noir if something lighter was desired. We went with a third, Reserve Red, a blend of cabernet sauvignon, merlot and cabernet blanc. Good choice. Eating quickly is not encouraged here and this wine was a gustatory reminder.

We tried only one dessert, bread pudding. It's different. It's served in a wine glass and is layered with fresh whipped cream. Oh, the best part? The Riesling glaze. We're not saying this getaway to Thunder Hill and Ferrante's is golf heaven, but if it were, we'd lead better lives.

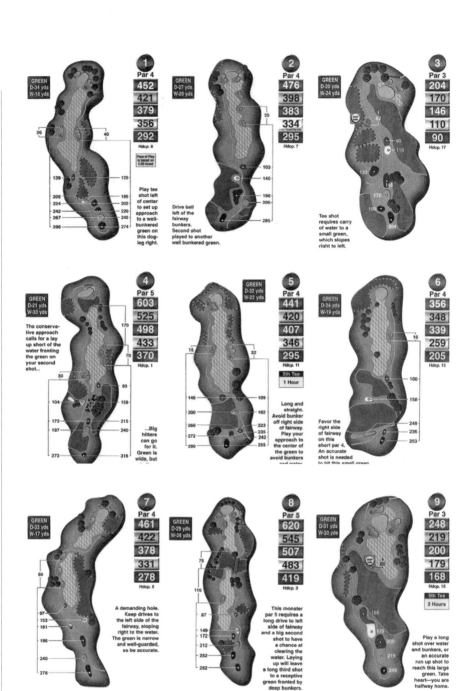

1 Par 4
GREEN
D-34 yds
W-18 yds

452
421
379
356
292
Hdcp. 9

Pace of Play is based on 4:30 round

26 · 40
139 · 123
205 · 185
224 · 202
242 · 220
267 · 245
296 · 274

Play tee shot left of center to set up approach to a well-bunkered green on this dog-leg right.

2 Par 4
GREEN
D-27 yds
W-29 yds

476
398
383
334
295
Hdcp. 7

55
103
140
190
206
285

Drive ball left of the fairway bunkers. Second shot played to another well bunkered green.

3 Par 3
GREEN
D-20 yds
W-24 yds

204
170
146
110
90
Hdcp. 17

62
90
110
133
170
190
204

Tee shot requires carry of water to a small green, which slopes right to left.

4 Par 5
GREEN
D-21 yds
W-33 yds

603
525
498
433
370
Hdcp. 1

The conservative approach calls for a lay up short of the water fronting the green on your second shot...

170
70
30
83
104
158
172
215
197
240
273
316

...Big hitters can go for it. Green is wide, but

5 Par 4
GREEN
D-32 yds
W-22 yds

441
420
407
346
295
Hdcp. 11

5th Tee
1 Hour

15 · 32
146 · 109
200 · 162
260 · 223
272 · 235
290 · 242
255

Long and straight. Avoid bunker off right side of fairway. Play your approach to the center of the green to avoid bunkers and water.

6 Par 4
GREEN
D-24 yds
W-19 yds

356
348
339
259
205
Hdcp. 13

16
100
158
248
236
253

Favor the right side of fairway on this short par 4. An accurate shot is needed to hit this small green.

7 Par 4
GREEN
D-33 yds
W-17 yds

461
422
378
331
278
Hdcp. 5

50
97
153
161
196
240
278

A demanding hole. Keep drives to the left side of the fairway, sloping right to the water. The green is narrow and well-guarded, so be accurate.

8 Par 5
GREEN
D-29 yds
W-28 yds

620
545
507
483
419
Hdcp. 3

75
115
87
149
172
212
252
282

This monster par 5 requires a long drive to left side of fairway and a big second shot to have a chance at clearing the water. Laying up will leave a long third shot to a receptive green fronted by deep bunkers.

9 Par 3
GREEN
D-31 yds
W-30 yds

248
219
200
179
168
Hdcp. 15

9th Tee
2 Hours

80
168
179
200
219
248

Play a long shot over water and bunkers, or an accurate run up shot to reach this large green. Take heart—you are halfway home.

Thunder Hill

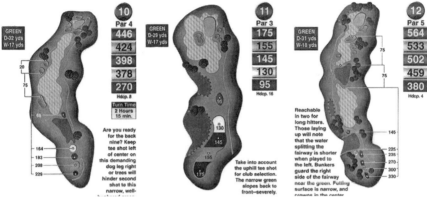

10
Par 4

GREEN
D-32 yds
W-17 yds

446
424
398
378
270

Hdcp. 8

Turn Time
2 Hours
15 min.

Are you ready for the back nine? Keep tee shot left of center on this demanding dog leg right or trees will hinder second shot to this narrow, well-

11
Par 3

GREEN
D-29 yds
W-17 yds

175
155
145
130
95

Hdcp. 16

Take into account the uphill tee shot for club selection. The narrow green slopes back to front—severely.

12
Par 5

GREEN
D-31 yds
W-18 yds

564
533
502
459
380

Hdcp. 4

Reachable in two for long hitters. Those laying up will note that the water splitting the fairway is shorter when played to the left. Bunkers guard the right side of the fairway near the green. Putting surface is narrow, and crowns in the center.

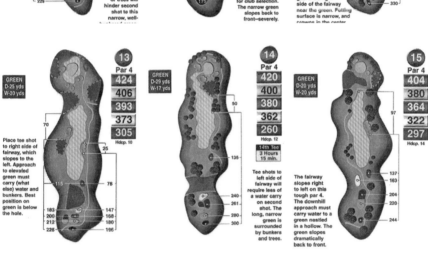

13
Par 4

GREEN
D-25 yds
W-20 yds

424
406
393
373
305

Hdcp. 10

Place tee shot to right side of fairway, which slopes to the left. Approach to elevated green must carry (what else) water and bunkers. Best position on green is below the hole.

14
Par 4

GREEN
D-29 yds
W-17 yds

420
400
380
362
260

Hdcp. 12

14th Tee
3 Hours
15 min.

Tee shots to left side of fairway will require less of a water carry on second shot. The long, narrow green is surrounded by bunkers and trees.

15
Par 4

GREEN
D-20 yds
W-20 yds

404
380
364
322
297

Hdcp. 14

The fairway slopes right to left on this tough par 4. The downhill approach must carry water to a green nestled in a hollow. The green slopes dramatically back to front.

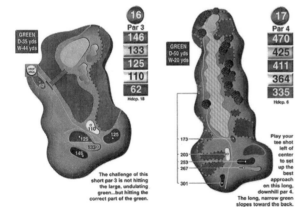

16
Par 3

GREEN
D-35 yds
W-44 yds

146
133
125
110
62

Hdcp. 18

The challenge of this short par 3 is not hitting the large, undulating green...but hitting the correct part of the green.

17
Par 4

GREEN
D-50 yds
W-20 yds

470
425
411
364
335

Hdcp. 6

Play your tee shot left of center to set to set up the best approach on this long, downhill par 4. The long, narrow green slopes toward the back.

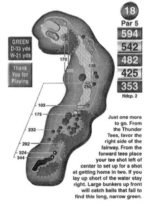

18
Par 5

GREEN
D-33 yds
W-21 yds

594
542
482
425
353

Hdcp. 2

Thank You for Playing

Just one more to go. From the Thunder Tees, favor the right side of the fairway. From the forward tees place your tee shot left of center to set up for a shot at getting home in two. If you lay up short of the water stay right. Large bunkers up front will catch balls that fail to find this long, narrow green.

KENNSINGTON GOLF CLUB

4171 Westford Pl.
Canfield
330.533.8733
www.kennsingtongolf.com

HOLIDAY INN BOARDMAN

7410 South Ave.
Boardman
330.726.1611

RESERVE RUN GOLF COURSE

625 East Western Reserve Rd.
Poland
330.758.1017

Getaways to the **Holiday Inn Boardman** have two elements not found elsewhere: Dan Walsh and Reserve Run Golf Course. We first met Walsh ten years or so ago. He had been transferred from Pennsylvania to Boardman. His reputation was sterling for creating golf outings, and the Holiday Inn in Boardman wasn't doing much. It didn't take him long. No figures are kept, but his percentage of repeat business has to be among the highest in the land. Guys who have been going to him for years now bring their sons.

That getaway of years ago remained with us. Great accommodations, best meal, long selection of very good courses, and ice cream.

Ice cream? Walsh had pointed out Handel's ice cream shop. It was across the street. It had just been named one of America's best by *USA Today*. We walked over before we left town, asked what the most popular ice cream was and then, taking the advice of the soda jerk, ordered double scoops of chocolate almond. Funny what details will stay with you.

That was dessert, however ill-timed; dinner the night before stayed with us, as well. It was a steak salad and just as we had it long ago, we had it again on our recent pilgrimage. TJ's Restaurant, in the hotel, wins so many awards, it has excused itself from some of the area competition. No sense being a bully.

Steak salad might not sound like much, but we found it, then and now, the best meal for players. They start by filling a very large salad bowl with all sorts of green, yellow, and red raw vegetables, the same ones our mothers insisted were good for us. On top of that is a pile of freshly-fried potatoes and on top of that, a perfectly grilled and sliced strip steak. Add two or three beers to that and you've just covered all the major food groups. Management also suggests the Youngstown Sports Grill, just down the street. If you become fall down drunk, there is a television in the floor.

We're getting ahead of ourselves. The getaway here began in the hotel parking lot, where we watched guys on a small crane remove the old Holiday Inn sign and replace it with a sign with the new logo.

If you become fall down drunk, there is a television in the floor.

We struck up a conversation with the crew boss, believing him to be part of a contractor company. Wrong. He was Gino Genova, chief engineer for the hotel, and as soon as he explained the new sign and logo, he launched into a soliloquy about his place of employment, including, but not limited to, the awards won by the restaurant and the Torchbearer Award, one of the company accolades that is given to only a few of its more than 2,000 hotels.

Geez. Whoever expected an engineer to also be the hotel proselytizer?

It didn't stop there. Just about everyone in Walsh's office had been there for more than a decade, and some, lots more. They are de facto aunts and uncles for each other's children, as close as brothers and sisters, and, most important to us, committed to the cause.

It didn't stop there, either. Walsh does getaways for women. This is true. One group is known as The Ladies From Canton. The other is the Cloverbelles from Pittsburgh. The former sounds like an Agatha Christie novel and the latter like the championship clogging team from Mercer County.

Walsh said the men come to play golf, drink whiskey, and have a real good time. The women are also interested in real good times (sometimes more), but Walsh added shopping.

Walsh offers a long list of very good courses for getaways. It's important and noteworthy that Walsh loves the game and loves to play. If you want to talk golf with this guy, you have an erudite pal for your palaver.

This year (2010), he's adding Knoll Run, in Struthers, to his golf buffet. We had time to play only two: the new Kennsington Golf Course in Canfield, and the knockout new Reserve Run Golf Course in Poland. Next time we go, we'll plan better and play all of them; on Walsh's list are eleven courses, including a few we've played before and can recommend without hesitation: Mill Creek, the 36-hole layout designed by the old Scotsman, Donald Ross and Yankee Run, which is one of our all time favorites, not just because we love the course, but the family too, the McMullins. Third generation if you can believe it.

(If there is a natural law we finally came to accept, it is this: Play from the proper tee. 'Nuff said.)

Here's something you expect from your getaway hotel: accurate tee times. Walsh isn't perfect, but in our experience, he's never missed. Not only does he make sure the tee time is registered, he provides specific driving instructions (although when he cautioned, "Wear your seat belts," we thought he went a bit over the top). He knows the traffic flows, too, so you'll get there on time.

Kennsington Golf Club was built as a CC, and it shows in the design and maintenance. Stimp? Rarely faster than 10.5, but with a few of the big greens, we sometimes got on the dance floor but couldn't hear the band. Excellent practice facilities.

This is another Brian Huntley gem and when he first looked around, maybe he got lost. Thick woods, great changes in elevation, enough water to keep the ol' retriever lubed and in the bag.

Talk about great neighbors; the course is bordered by the Kyle Woods Nature Preserve on the east and on the south by Camp Stambaugh, a Boy Scout camp.

If you want to play it from the tips, it's 7,044, and remember, par is 71. There are five sets of tees. That's bent grass throughout. Love the bunkering, mostly because it defines the hole for first-time players. The ride is up and down, around the bend, and gorgeous. Water, often in the form of streams, tightens things up. It's gorgeous. How could it not be?

Kennsington opened mid-season, 2006, and it will take another year or two for it to settle in, though mid- and high-handicappers, like us, will never notice.

First surprise shows up at No. 2, which has a fairway wider than the lapels on your old man's tuxedo. There is, however, the matter of the stand of trees in the middle of the fairway. It is Augusta's Eisenhower Tree taken to the next level. Most high-handicappers aim for the middle of the stand, confident in their inability to hit a straight drive. More often than not, they're rewarded with what appears to be a good drive.

Before we forget, the wind is another factor here. On both finishing holes, a north wind will make the second shot a long one. Especially 18, where players might hit a driver and short iron one day and then driver and 3-wood on another.

Lots of memorable holes, but No. 7 is where we left a perfectly good sleeve of Titleists. Huntley knew that when we approached the tee for the first time, we would stop in our tracks, stare, and then, with a low whistle, say something along the lines of, "Holy Moly."

A dogleg to right, it has bunkering in the elbow, trees on both sides, a ravine that gives pause, and a small lake going down one side. Did we add it's 420 from the whites? Did we add the hole plays uphill? We did? Okay, that's all the help we can be.

The home hole. Walk off 18 with a par and you can say, what a great hole; walk off with more than four and you probably lost the match.

It plays only 385 from the whites, but *what* a 385. It is a memorable finishing hole, one that stays with us, a hole worth study and strategy. Bunkering on the right side of the fairway, a green surrounded by water on three sides, and a green with not one, not two, but three tiers. To add some more challenge, Huntley used up all his leftover sand to make five bunkers on the left side. If the flag is in the top right, rub your prayer beads while selecting a club.

Round Number Two we played at **Reserve Run Golf Course**. We'd heard good things about the place, but this was our first trip around this new track. It is another Ohio course built on land that has been quarried.

Walk out of the clubhouse and a great view of the course is there. The big body of water is the quarry, almost 100 feet deep in spots, the source of all the water used on the course. Lots of springs feed it, clear and cold. Largemouth bass, blue gill, and crappie, if you have your Ronco Pocket Fisherman in your bag. Also, on the course are fox, coyote, deer and wild turkey. Not likely Ronco will come out with a pocket shotgun.

Reserve opened in 1999; it took one year to build and was designed by Barry Serafin. Six par 3s, three on each side. Great finishing hole is number one handicap, a 440-yard par 4, uphill.

Speed bumps in the driveway. They weren't part of the original design, but arriving players eager to change shoes drove a bit too fast.

At this point, the record is held by two guys, who carded 64s. What a pleasure it would have been to caddy for either.

The course almost looks as if Mother Nature designed it, and an argument could be made. She was the first and most influential.

Bent grass fairways, tee boxes and greens. Excellent drainage. They used plenty of handsome stone on the course. Water is an important fact on five holes and the wind is a constant hazard. The greens are USGA-design sand greens. If all you've played is pushups, get ready for some golf pleasure. The Stimpmeter reads 10.5 or 11. When it's time to top-dress them, only one half of the green is done at a time. That means no more "two putts and pick it up." Drat!

Just about every hole here would work well for a postcard. No. 7, a short par 4, is picturesque with the quarry running down its left side. It's a slight dogleg to the right and has a generous landing area, but the terrain on the right side shoots up, so, missing the short grass can be worrisome. Turn around and you see the entire length of the quarry lake. Deep woods down the right side and the course on the left.

Seven, eight and nine pretty much define Reserve Run. No. 8 is all carry, it's the end of the reservoir, a par 3 with stone walls and a shallow and wide green. No. 9 is a blind tee shot and straight up. It doesn't stop. No. 10 from an elevated tee then rises, then takes a very sharp dogleg left. All of it beautiful, very well manicured, and, from the proper tees, a challenge and a joy.

Kennsington

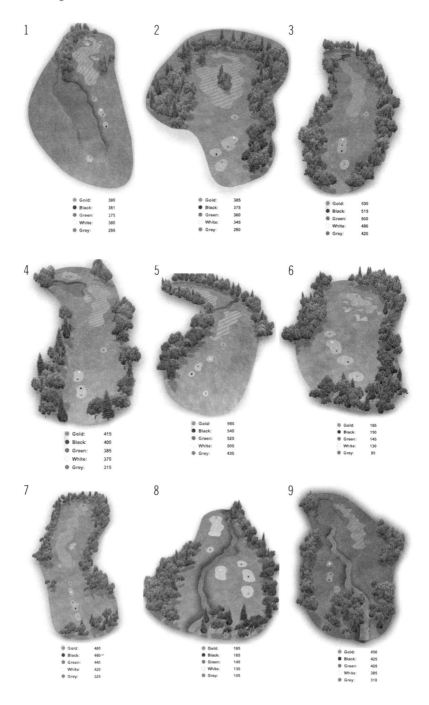

1

Gold:	390
Black:	381
Green:	375
White:	360
Grey:	295

2

Gold:	385
Black:	375
Green:	360
White:	345
Grey:	280

3

Gold:	530
Black:	515
Green:	500
White:	480
Grey:	420

4

Gold:	415
Black:	400
Green:	385
White:	370
Grey:	315

5

Gold:	565
Black:	540
Green:	525
White:	505
Grey:	435

6

Gold:	185
Black:	150
Green:	145
White:	130
Grey:	95

7

Gold:	480
Black:	460
Green:	440
White:	420
Grey:	325

8

Gold:	195
Black:	165
Green:	145
White:	135
Grey:	105

9

Gold:	450
Black:	425
Green:	405
White:	385
Grey:	310

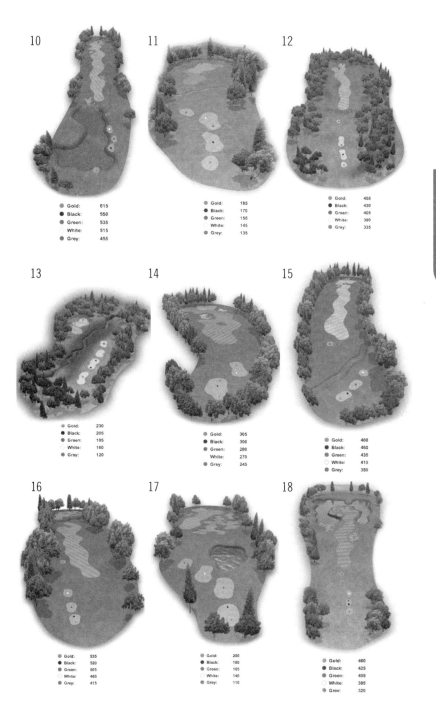

10

Gold:	615
Black:	550
Green:	535
White:	515
Grey:	455

11

Gold:	185
Black:	170
Green:	155
White:	145
Grey:	135

12

Gold:	455
Black:	430
Green:	405
White:	390
Grey:	335

13

Gold:	230
Black:	205
Green:	185
White:	160
Grey:	120

14

Gold:	305
Black:	300
Green:	290
White:	270
Grey:	245

15

Gold:	480
Black:	460
Green:	435
White:	410
Grey:	350

16

Gold:	535
Black:	520
Green:	505
White:	485
Grey:	415

17

Gold:	200
Black:	180
Green:	165
White:	140
Grey:	110

18

Gold:	460
Black:	425
Green:	405
White:	385
Grey:	320

WINDMILL LAKES GOLF CLUB

6544 SR 14

Ravenna

330.297.0440

www.golfwindmilllakes.com

ROCKING HORSE INN

248 West Riddle Ave.

Ravenna

800.457.0439

www.rockinghorseinn.net

ARNIE'S WEST BRANCH STEAK HOUSE

5343 State Route 14

Ravenna

330.297.1717

There are those among us who couldn't care less about a rich single malt, or the long odds of drawing to an inside straight, but whose passion and regard for the Royal and Ancient is second to none.

Are there getaways for them?

Surely you jest. You're in Ohio, for goodness sakes. In the state that sent to tournaments Weiskopf, Cook, and Nicklaus; whose Buckeyes so dominate Michigan that the game is now known as a warm up for tougher opponents; who produced, elected, jailed and then hired as a radio personality Jim Traficant. A better question might be, how many getaways are there for these sober, financially competent, trunk slammers, and the answer is: How many do you need?

One is in Ravenna.

Ah, Ravenna, named after the lovely Italian city on the Adriatic coast, and on this side of the pond, home to the Ravenna Arsenal.

We found lodging so elegant, so comfortable, so peaceful, that men have been known to be late for tee times. And arriving late for a tee time at Windmill Lakes golf course is apostasy.

Windmill Lakes Golf Club is Kent State University's home course. Tour player Jon Mills also learned there at the hands of the master, Coach Page. Herb Page is worth a book of his own; as one of the most successful and honored golf coaches in NCAA history, on his calling card should be humility and gratitude. It's just the way he is and has always been. If you come across him at the course, by all means shake hands and thank him. (He's the short guy walking fast.) For the rest of your born days, it allows you to do the routine, "Shake the hand that shook the hand of …"

Scary-looking bunker in the front of the green looks, from a distance, like the Cheshire Cat with a frown.

The pro shop is crowded with merchandise and equipment. *Note bene: Before the Christmas holidays, its sale is one of the best.*

On the course, the terrain rolls gently and there's no trickery. Lots of demands but it's all honest. It opened in 1970, and Windmill may be the most challenging for its relentless par 4s. There is but a single par 5 on the front and back, so it's big par 4s matched with big greens. If you can putt out in regulation or better, you're either a single- digit handicap or a sandbagger.

It's not over-bunkered, and there's nothing sneaky about them. What you see is what you get. Forty sand bunkers rest here along with seven lakes. The bunkers won't cripple your chance of par, but will provide a serious sprain. Every water hazard looks as if it belongs there.

Choose your tee with humility and hope, not bravado.

The first hole is a good example. Almost 400 yards for us and it's a great driving hole, but the ball has to settle on the left side of the fairway lest the approach be ambushed by trees. And this first green is indicative of the size and shape of the greens here. *(Reminded us that maintaining large greens is time-consuming as well as costly.)*

No. 4 is the par 5 on this side, a straightaway of 521 yards for us, with stands of trees on both sides of the fairway. Another hazard can be the creek that is on the right and has been known to swallow up poorly hit approaches.

No. 9 is only 377 yards for us, but it's the number three handicap hole, which should raise a flag or two on the tee. We had to fly a bunker to get on, where we were promptly fooled and fooled again by the green.

It doesn't slow up on No. 10, where accuracy off the tee is the best way to snag a par here. Trees tighten the fairway of this little dogleg, and maintaining the pressure is a green that is the fraternal twin to No. 9. Two consecutive greens where one of us said, "If it weren't for the speed and direction, I'da hadda great putt."

This side's par 5 is No. 16 and isn't long, but again, demands accuracy off the tee and beyond. Scary-looking bunker in the front of the green looks, from a distance, like the Cheshire Cat with a frown.

We had to wait a couple minutes on the seventeenth tee, and one of us had a particularly astute observation of Windmill: It is more challenging than it looks, it's worth playing two consecutive rounds, and how did we fail to score better, given the yardage from the regular tees, only a chip longer than 6,100 yards? Answering his own question, he said, "Three words: Putt, putt and putt." Which reminded us of Chi-Chi Rodriguez, who thought putting should be restricted to two shots, then pick up and head to the next tee box. Except he said it with more vigor.

Great home hole. A straightway par 4 to an elevated green, it plays 380 yards for mortals. It's easy to see where you're going: it's right through that tunnel of trees and woe to the man whose ball ricochets off a sturdy ash.

We found **Rocking Horse Inn** in Ravenna. Nearby avenues are named Chestnut, Maple Lane, Hickory, Sycamore, and Spruce. The place isn't big until you add in the porch, a big, wide, deep, wrap-around with wicker chairs and furniture.

Not to drop names, but how would you like to play where British Open champion Ben Curtis honed his skills? True. Long before he took on Royal St. George and the best talent in the world, he was in khaki shorts, listening to KSU golf coach Herb Page.

We knew a second round was in order, but we passed on it and headed for home, in this case, the Rocking Horse Inn, there to soak our bruises, assuage our egos and read the financial section of *The Times*.

By the way, construction for the Rocking Horse started in 1867. Exactly one century later, Nicklaus and Palmer were going at it for the U.S. Open at Baltusrol, in New Jersey. A coincidence? Maybe, but we think not.

The name of the inn comes from the previous owner, a woman who loved antiques and glass. The current innkeeper is Robert Walker, whose other work is as a Ravenna fireman and EMT. The place has been his pride and joy for eight years. Rocking Horse is a Victorian mansion and the architectural style is called Stick Style.

Four rooms are available. Hmmm. Four players make a foursome. Another coincidence? Maybe, but we think not.

Get up as early or as late as you want. The continental breakfast is put out at 6 a.m., and replenished until noon. Plenty of coffee, hot chocolate, tea, juice, plus a mess of cereals, bagels, breads and fresh-made cake bread.

Here are two features not usually bragged about on getaways: a library and a piano. In addition to the rooms, a suite is also available. The four rooms are named for women: Julianne, Paula, Anne, and Victoria. Antiques abound.

We went to **Arnie's West Branch Steak House**. Next time we go to Arnie's, we'll either get there earlier or pass on weekends. The guy does one heck of a trade on Fridays and Saturdays. Very friendly, very good steaks prepared with a minimum of fuss. Arnie's is the sort of place your old man took you for graduation or dinner before you left for Marine boot camp.

Windmill Lakes Golf Club

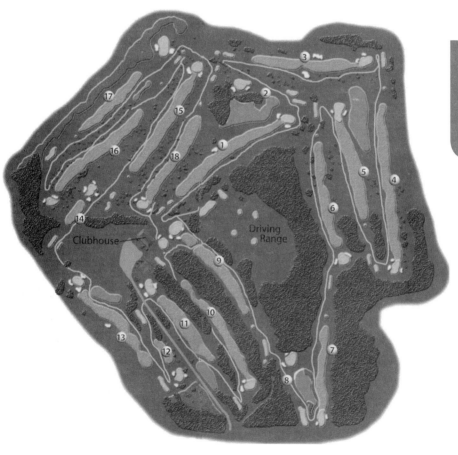

Clubhouse

Driving Range

HEMLOCK SPRINGS GOLF CLUB
4654 Cork Cold Springs Rd.
Geneva
440.466.4044

THE LODGE AND CONFERENCE CENTER AT GENEVA-ON-THE-LAKE
4888 N Broadway
Geneva-on-the-Lake
866.806.8066
www.thelodgeatgeneva.com

Geneva-on-the-Lake is The Town That Father Time Forgot. Would that He forgot a few more. This place is a blast. A few decades ago, it was the stomping grounds for outlaw bikers (no pun intended), which made people-watching far more interesting than any pole dancer. The town brags that many decades before, its guests included Harvey Firestone and John D. Rockefeller.

It is a summer town, a walking town, a small resort on the lake, and the strip is lined with one-story, owner-operated businesses—saloons, hamburger and pizza joints, souvenir shops, arcade games, and topped off with signage that makes garish look gorgeous. It is genuine, All-American, the antithesis of Disney World, and the fun, if it got any better, I'd need two faces for this smile.

To serve the summer crowd, lots and lots of cottages were built on the lake, everything from plain and simple to pretty nice to splurge-worthy, all helped by the greatest background, Lake Erie. Our shallow Great Lake provides perch and walleye along with beaches.

Want to think you died and went to heaven? Settle into an Adirondack chair, choice of booze in one hand, choice of tobacco in the other, and watch as the sun sets. Mother Nature's lullaby is waves lapping at the shore.

While we didn't stay in any of the cottages, we toured a couple, and cottage life here is very, very appealing. We stayed at the **Lodge and Conference Center at Geneva-on-the-Lake,** which doesn't intrude on the lake as much as it partners with it; like two old pals, neither imposes on the other. Plus it has a bar and restaurant, the best in beds, all the hot water you need to shower, and comfortable accommodations when one of the guys yells, "Shut up and deal."

While the area has a long history, the Lodge isn't even 10 years old. If we had to describe the architectural style, we would say restrained.

Whoa, back up to the dinner table. The main restaurant is Horizons and the outdoor dining is the Terrace. While we've been partial to drinking outdoors since we were 15, having dinner al fresco never interested us. Call us unsophisticated, but the idea of competing with airborne insects for our entrees put the kibosh on the idea. And anyway, at Horizons, there are white tablecloths, upholstered chairs, and great views of, well, the horizon.

From the first tee, the hole is defined and the path to par is clear. Of course not all of us can take that path...

The chef here does a wonderful job with pasta, and we're not talking spaghetti and meatballs. One of us had the chicken and shrimp alfredo because, he said, it's the most difficult sauce to make well. There's a balance, he said, between creamy and too thick, flavor that has to be full, but not cloying. And the pasta has to be perfectly cooked. That green stuff on his plate? Spinach fettuccini. We knew it was good because he refused to share. A chef would understand that to be a compliment; we thought, after his lecture on the dish, samples would be offered. We thought wrong.

It's not as if the rest of us went hungry. The most flavorful dish on our table was also the most healthy: salmon with a teriyaki sauce.

Nothing wrong with the pork medallions, either, served up, as they were with spaetzles. We were impressed with the service, though we couldn't figure out why. We think it was the professionalism of the server, which we define as anticipating every need or request, yet never getting in the way.

For those of us who don't wake up and have coffee while watching the show that is Lake Erie, it can be mesmerizing. Lake Erie is downright enchanting at that hour. Fishermen and sailors are on the lake, gulls sweeping and turning, families are making their way to the beach.

But duty calls.

We came to play **Hemlock Springs Golf Club**, which is gearing up for its fiftieth anniversary. Not only do we enjoy the course, but *Golf Digest* has flung a fistful of stars at it, and the Cleveland Browns alumni play here every year as part of a fund-raiser for United Appeal.

Tee times here are ten minutes apart, which adds more fun to the game than cart girls. Ben Zink, who did Chardon Lakes GC, designed the course in 1961 and current owners have been at it for more than thirty years. One more little thing: If this course isn't the cleanest, we'll spring for the next box of Handi-Wipes. It's as if management here has a litter crew combing the grounds every few hours. That dedication to the small stuff extends to the big stuff. We think that after perfectly mowing a fairway, the guy on the tractor stands up, looks at his work, and says, "Now *that* is a fairway."

If putting is your strength, this is the place to show off. The practice green is just like the greens on the course and after playing two or three holes, the good putters in the group say to themselves, "Holy cats, where have these babies been all my life?" More true than your mistress, and maintained just as well or better. Make sure when leaving the green the flag is all the way in, your ball marks are restored, bunkers raked and the wrapper from your Padron 3000 is in either your pocket or heading for the trash can.

We like the way the course begins because No. 1 shows off lots of Hemlock's strengths. Hemlock gives good directions. From the first tee, the hole is defined and the path to par is clear. Of course not all of us can take that path, and the definition of the hole offers us alternate routes. A 379-yard par 4, a creek runs across at 265 yards, well out of reach for us, but giving pause to the big hitters in the group. The green is accessible, but it's elevated and sand hazards are on both sides. So? How close to the water do you want to get?

Management brags that No. 11, a par 3 from an elevated green, is its signature hole, and we agree. Sort of. One hundred eighty-six yards from the whites; on no other tee does anticipation run so high. Trees line the hole, water precedes the elevated green and sand on both sides provides further directions. A ball struck well on this tee is a source of pleasure; a poorly-struck ball is the ignition for all sorts of bad words. There is only one chance to do it right.

No. 12 tee is where we talked about the skills of the mower. Just a beautiful par 4, and only 306 from the whites, but a narrow landing area and water on the right. The fairway rolls down from the tee, and rolls back up to the green. A short par 4, to be sure, but the players who score par or better here are accurate off the tee and precise iron players.

It took us three good shots, the third being a lob wedge, on No. 15, a par 5 that begins with an uphill tee shot and bends to the right. Only 469 from the whites, missing any shot means getting your knuckles rapped by the Great Goddess of Golf.

We played the home hole, a 551-yard par 5, from the tips. So this is what The Champ was looking at finishing his record round. His record was safe with us. From the tee, big water on the right and, later, a little squirt a yard and a half out.

Jimmy Hanlin PGA is the director of golf at Little Mountain Country Club and is an owner of Stonewater Golf Club, and the Woven Trail. Over the course of his career, he has put together golf outings enough to stretch to the moon and back.

He says putting together an outing is like working on a jigsaw puzzle. Looks great when it's finished, but if there is one missing piece, that's what draws attention.

Hanlin can control parking, tee times, prizes, contests, dinner; he can control just about everything except the weather.

Same for The Guy.

Hanlin says that while every detail, and The Guy will agree with this, is important, none is more important than food.

If Tlaloc, the Aztec god of rain, decides to soak the fairways and greens, and maybe add a few grace notes with lightning and thunder, none but the foolish and suicidal is going to tee it up. Golfers understand that. Oh, they grumble and groan, but they understand that.

Hanlin is not going to be blamed for bad weather, as he might be for slow greens, a starter with liquor on his breath, malfunctioning carts, or inaccurate scoring.

If weather closes down the course, it is Hanlin's responsibility to commiserate and provide rain passes so everyone in the outing will be able to return and play the course. He is going to make sure everyone enjoys dinner and drinks.

But bad food? Whoa—when that happens, the course is first remembered for bad food. It puts a chilling effect on the business of future outings.

Hanlin says if the course can't be played, the outing can enjoy drinks and visiting as well as a very good meal. Players walk away feeling good about the place.

There is a corollary with golf getaways. Food is the source of energy and pleasure. What other subject can be so described? We mean besides cocaine.

When we're on the road, the only thing that can faster cripple us is a drunk driver going left of center. So, like the jigsaw puzzle, eating is a vital piece of the package.

It's a good thing the Great Goddess of Golf blessed men with simple, yet sophisticated, tastes in food. It can be summed up in three words: Steak and taters.

Throughout research for this book, we enjoyed steak and taters more than any other dish, and we started and finished the tour without problems. But in some towns there are tried-and-true dishes that we tried and greatly enjoyed.

Here are a couple tips we developed that have served us well: Call the restaurant before going. Reservations are a good idea; having to wait in the lounge for an hour is a bad idea. If the service is good, tip heavy. It is not going to make the waiter or waitress rich and it's not going to make you poor. But both parties will feel good about it. Ask questions. The one that worked best for us was asked of the waiter. We said, "If you were having dinner here tonight, what would you have?" He or she is not going to steer you wrong.

Speaking of the Aztecs, what could be worse on a getaway than the rumble of Montezuma's Revenge?

THE SANCTUARY
GOLF CLUB
2017 Applegrove St. NW

North Canton

330.499.7721

www.thesanctuarygolf.com

HILTON GARDEN
INN
5251 Landmark Blvd.

North Canton

330.966.4907

HANDEL'S
HOMEMADE ICE
CREAM
2041 East Maple St.

North Canton

330.244.9200

BRAVO CUCINA ITALIANA
4224 Everhard Rd. NW

Canton

330.494.9170

The Sanctuary Golf Club. That has to be one of the best names for
a golf course. Here, the entire staff wears Franciscan monks' robes,
speaks in Gregorian chant, and forgives just about every sin except
failing to repair divots and ball marks.

Just kidding. But this North Canton course does try to live up
to its name, and does it pretty well. It can play as long as 6,811 yards
or as short as 4,921 yards. Between the opening and home holes is a
wonderful trip and great example of parkland golf. It's Brian Huntley's
work, and his designs in Ohio are one reason Buckeye golf is so good.
(Although where he got this idea to make the first hole the most
resistant to par on the front side, we'll never know.)

But lots of water, including cattails and natural grasses, greens big
enough to offer a wealth of pin positions, and bent grass throughout.
The terrain pitches and rolls (same with these gorgeous greens), and
Huntley had lots of ground to work with; it's not a walking course, but

it's permissible.

Landing areas are sometimes generous, sometimes tempting. And holes framed by woods are always a delight. There are no tricked up holes, but following the designer's advice works well here. Huntley shows us just where we should go. If—and it's a big if—we're launching from the proper tee, this is a course where you find yourself smiling, yet not aware of it.

It's quiet here and that's no surprise. The course is made more attractive with flower beds on the tees.

Practice green here, though no range. On the first tee is a practice net if it's necessary to hit a couple balls before teeing it up. Maybe those couple balls should be hit with a fairway wood or hybrid. Bringing out the howitzer this early in the battle can put a damper on the game. On this opening hole, straight is far more important than long. Unless you're an old artilleryman and know what you're doing. (Hey, Napoleon thought he knew what he was doing, too.)

Five sets of tees and moving up one tee for the first round is a good idea. You have often seen us walk to the tips, look at the hole, then come back to play from the whites. We do that because it's a visual pleasure to see what the designer laid out for the very low handicap players.

Back to No. 1, the most challenging hole on this side. From the waybacks, it will kill you: 455 yards to a fairway hemmed in by trees on both sides and o.b. on the left. From the black tees, however, it plays 380 yards. See? With a fairway wood, it's not so scary. Plus, it's going downhill anyhow. The blacks play 6,109 yards. For carnivores, the penultimate tee is silver, and it plays 6,442 yards.

Not only do we enjoy big greens, but we appreciate the additional costs to maintain them. We enjoy them because they can be game-breakers. The difference between a two-putt and a four-putt often wins matches. Ask any touring pro. These greens have been nurtured since 2002, so if you think you see the line, you probably do.

Just a quick aside: We treat all greens as if they were hallowed ground. Because they are. We don't rest the lighted end of a cigar on them, we don't pick up the wedge by stepping on it, we set the flag down instead of tossing it, and we repair our own ball marks along with one or two more.

To speed play, we also putt out unless someone else is in our line. That's one of two time-saving techniques we wish Congress would make into law. (It's not as if they're doing anything else.) The other is honors on the green. Yeah, yeah, we know it's traditional, but we play, "first on the tee, first to hit," and it allows us to play faster.

Walking off the first green with a par is cause for celebration, however muted. And the next hole is pure fun: a par 3 with a green that can be diabolical. But landing a short iron *on the proper part of the green* is cause for fist bumps. Landing it above the flag, and putting downhill? Hmmm. Squeeze the prayer beads before taking the club head back.

The first par 5 is No. 3, and even the better players with us didn't like the bet for eagle. A dogleg right, but with too much sand for the gamble. Better a three-shotter with a chance at par or birdie.

No. 4 is another tee box where judgment trumps valor. Only 311 yards from our tees, but the real challenge comes on the green. By this time, we were comfortable knowing the speed of the green, and here's a green where speed is more important than direction. You've been warned.

Beginning on No. 6, water takes its cue and in addition to making the course beautiful, it better defines holes and the shots that are necessary.

The back side begins with a wet and sandy par 5, only 519 yards. (Did we say "only?" Sorry.) For those of us who found the par 3, No. 9, to be an ambush, No. 10 is a hole to either 1.) get well or 2.) start sending distress messages.

The back side comes to a glorious finish with a straightaway par 4, 418 yards from the black tees.

If the hunger pangs must be sated, either at the turn or after the match, the grill is outdoors. Dixie Lee runs the place and if you can't get along with Dixie Lee, you should be under house arrest.

But if you can hold off, we recommend **Handel's Homemade**

Ice Cream for some of the best ice cream on this planet. The first time we had it was in Boardman, and we went at our hotelier's recommendation. Handel's makes its own ice cream, offers more choices than your insurance guy, and serves it up at a very good price. Our idea of the perfect appetizer.

We rested our weary bones at **Hilton Garden Inn**, which is only five years old and looks it. One guy has to get a suite, if money is to be exchanged over a few hands of poker.

Nice pool, very good service, comfortable rooms. But we like the location. It sits on I-77 and the Akron-Canton Airport. Highway noise can either lull you to sleep or keep you up, so make sure the light sleepers are housed on the airport side of the hotel. Breakfast is available, too.

But let's talk dinner. Who talks breakfast, anyway? Just a few minutes away, in Belden Village, is a very good Italian place, **Bravo Cucina Italiana**. We like it for more than one reason. It's white tablecloth, which always makes us feel special; it has a great menu, a few steaks and chops as well as pasta in many of its glorious manifestations; plus, you can spend a lot or a little. Before you make the mistake, the Bolognese sauce is not baloney in a red sauce. It is, however, a meat sauce, and wonderful on pasta. Even better, we thought, was the spaghetti and meatballs. Some of the best meatballs ever, these are made of a combination pork and beef. We ordered an extra plate of meatballs so everyone at the table could enjoy.

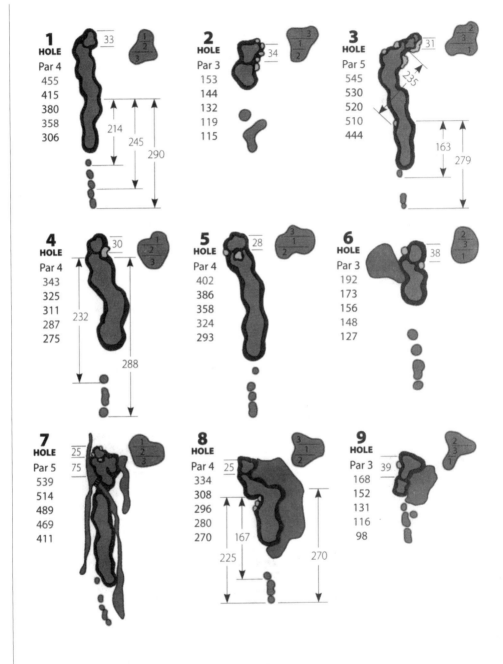

1 HOLE
Par 4
455
415
380
358
306

33

2 HOLE
Par 3
153
144
132
119
115

34

3 HOLE
Par 5
545
530
520
510
444

31
235
163
279

214
245
290

4 HOLE
Par 4
343
325
311
287
275

30
232
288

5 HOLE
Par 4
402
386
358
324
293

28

6 HOLE
Par 3
192
173
156
148
127

38

7 HOLE
Par 5
539
514
489
469
411

25
75

8 HOLE
Par 4
334
308
296
280
270

25
167
225
270

9 HOLE
Par 3
168
152
131
116
98

39

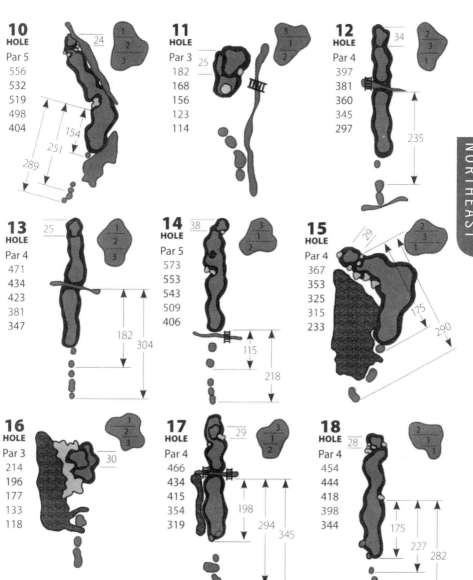

10 HOLE
Par 5
556
532
519
498
404

24

11 HOLE
Par 3
182
168
156
123
114

25

12 HOLE
Par 4
397
381
360
345
297

34

235

13 HOLE
Par 4
471
434
423
381
347

25

182
304

14 HOLE
Par 5
573
553
543
509
406

38

115
218

15 HOLE
Par 4
367
353
325
315
233

29
175
290

16 HOLE
Par 3
214
196
177
133
118

30

17 HOLE
Par 4
466
434
415
354
319

29
198
294
345

18 HOLE
Par 4
454
444
418
398
344

28
175
227
282

NORTHEAST

THE LEGENDS OF MASSILLON

2700 Augusta Dr. S.E.
Massillon
330.830.4653
www.thelegends.com

CARRABBA'S ITALIAN GRILL

6560 Strip Ave. NW
Canton
330.966.2426

HAMPTON INN

44 First St. SW
Massillon
330.834.1144

Boy, talk about your presumptuous: When Massillon city fathers (and mothers, we guess) decided, a decade and a half ago, to build and operate a first-class public golf course, they named it **The Legends of Massillon**. The Legends? There is the Legend of Sleepy Hollow, and both King Arthur and Robin Hood are legends. But a brand-new golf course in Massillon?

It doesn't stop there. Its address is on Augusta Drive. Now, Augusta is legendary.

You want a legend? We'll give you a legend: Paul Brown. The most influential man in the history of football went to high school here, played quarterback here, and after picking up a bachelor's and master's degree, coached here. You think the '69 Mets were amazin'? We'll give you amazin': 80-8-2 with his Tigers. He's buried at Rose Hill Cemetery here.

Methinks we protest too much, because on the other hand, the city went first class and who knows? Maybe before the century is out, it will have attained legendary status. Whether it does or not, we found it to be the perfect two-day, one-night getaway.

When management decided to expand the original Legends of Massillon from eighteen to twenty-seven holes, the operation looked like a three-card Monte game. Except everybody won. The original eighteen was split in three and to each six holes, a new package of three holes was added.

Opened in 1995, designed by Canadian John Robinson, owned and operated by City Hall, features bent grass throughout, big greens and a very nice clubhouse.

And for getaway purposes, what could be better than playing twenty-seven holes a couple days in a row? The whole place is beautiful, and Robinson, limited with elevation changes, made his track challenging with water and sand. Only five holes *don't* have water, and about eighty sand bunkers dot the layout.

Landing areas, by and large, are well defined, but it's not a big hitters course unless the big hitter is also accurate. If that's the case, there are eagles to be had here. Large greens and four sets of tees. One more time: Large greens. Very well maintained and at this point in their lives, nicely settled. The speed on the practice green matches the speed on the course; our guess is the Stimp rolls around a 10, and while the greens are not tricky, they ain't easy.

On No. 2, there should be a sign reading: "Don't be foolish, put that driver back where it belongs."

The nine-hole segments are South, East, and North. South begins benignly enough; a short 4 four and while close to the green a creek cuts across the fairway, the hole is made for pars and better. That's the way it goes—short and reachable holes, but every one with water and most with sand. Did we say this is three courses for shotmakers? If we didn't, we want to now. No. 8 is all solid ground and No. 9, pretty dry, but with excellent fairway bunkering.

North begins with more challenge, a dogleg right and big bunkers—right and left—to match. It's on this nine that John

Robinson's strength with bunkers is so evident. With the use of sand, he doesn't make the course penal, but he does insist that the ball go where you aim. With that feature alone, he makes the Legends a thinking man's course. Pin placement, of course, makes a difference throughout, and we wondered if anyone ever sought to determine the difference in scores with easy placements and difficult placements. We love No. 9, a buttonhook par 5 of 496 yards from the whites. Much of that yardage can be eliminated going for the green in two, but as you address that shot, you'll hear, in the back of your head, "Cast Your Fate to the Wind."

The East course begins with a 512-yard par 5, which is why we enjoy starting there. On in three, putt or two, and we're off to the races. Getting on in two is possible, though sand on both sides of the green might have something to say about that.

On No. 2, there should be a sign reading: "Don't be foolish, put that driver back where it belongs." It is here Robinson lays a trap: sand and water in abundance, yet it's a short par 4. The home hole, 327 yards from the whites, and don't let that water scare you.

As long as plans call for twenty-seven holes a day, stopping for breakfast is a good idea. Especially when the place is locally owned. Top of the Viaduct it's called and loading up on protein is a simple matter. Steak and eggs does just fine, so does the meat lovers omelet (are we not men?). If you're a pancake man, your language is spoken here. If your life of deprivation meant never enjoying sausage gravy and biscuits, throw caution to the wind. The stuff is so good you can see why cardiologists and other busybodies want to ban it. Top of the Viaduct opens at 6 a.m., bless its little country heart. With 160 seats, no waiting.

We enjoyed the **Hampton Inn** because it's downtown. Downtown Massillon rarely boosts the blood pressure ('cept when the Tigers are in town), but we love being able to just walk around, maybe enjoy a palaver with a local. Plus, the hotel is comfortable, clean as a whistle and when you ask for a wake-up call, say, at 5:30, that's the exact time the phone starts ringing.

For supper we jumped in the cars and headed over to nearby Belden Village, where there are enough restaurants to satisfy most every getaway palate. We settled in **Carrabba's Italian Grill** because we've gone there in other cities and are amazed with the quality and service. And this place is a chain? Geez, what if more chains were able to produce like this place? Plenty of pasta and lots of sauces. One of our less sophisticated said, "Boy, lots more than spaghetti and meatballs," as if that classic is unworthy. But the truth is, you can get a pasta dish here and brag about it when you get home, the variety of sauces, pastas and meat go from over there to way over there. Plus a dessert we didn't try, but has the locals salivating, the Chocolate Sonya. We would have, but if you clean your plate here, you're full. Very full. Try Sonya for us and let us know, will you?

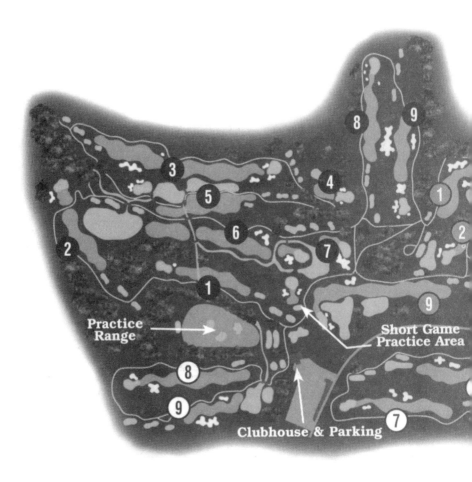

Practice Range

Short Game Practice Area

Clubhouse & Parking

The Legends of Massillon

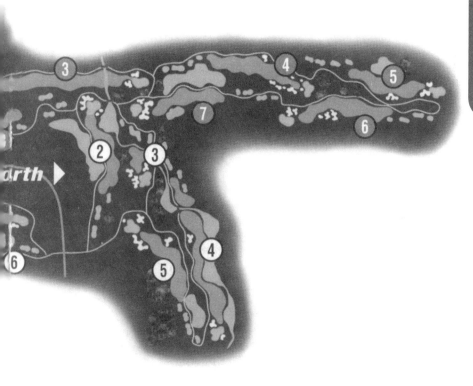

Packing for the Getaway

Getawayers have arrived without golf shoes, without belts, without adequate stores of cigars. One guy, practicing his short game in his backyard the night before, left his 9-iron propped up against the garage. As your Aunt Louise would say, "What were you thinking of?"

Packing for the trip should be one of the easier getaway chores. It's not as if we have to send a change of address card to the post office, or get referrals for a new dentist, for goodness' sakes. We'll only be gone a few days.

Some of the things we need at home can be forgotten when we go on getaways and the effects are negligible:

1. Nose and ear trimmers.
2. Pajamas.
3. Shaving gear.
4. Cell phones.
5. Handguns.

Other items, big ticket and small, just have to be packed lest there is a self-inflicted major or minor irritation. How can you concentrate on putting if, for example, you know the socks you're wearing are the same socks you'll wear tomorrow?

This is how we do it, and it has worked without fail for many years: Standing in the bedroom, we run through the mornings of the getaways:

1. First thing is pack the old kit bag: Toothpaste, toothbrush, aspirin, dental floss, nail trimmers, shave cream and razor. For those of us who are of a mind: denture cream, eye drops, prescription drugs, comb, ointments of any and all manner, deodorant.
2. Visualize getting dressed on the first day. First a shirt and it is tossed on the bed. Then underpants, tossed on top of the shirt. Then pants or shorts, on the same, growing pile. Going to slip a belt around your waist? Belt. Next are socks. Then shoes. Stop right there. Forget handkerchiefs? You did, didn't you?
3. And then ask yourself, if I shower after the match and before dinner, what do I need? Almost surely it's fresh undies, shirt and socks. 'Kay, all on the same pile.

4. Then repeat for every day of the getaway and brother, that's what goes into the suitcase.

5. Oh, one other thing: A laundry bag. As your sweaty, smelly, dirty clothes come off, they should go into the laundry bag and not piled in a corner.

   And this is how we pack the pouches on the golf bag, assuming first that there are no more than fourteen sticks in it:

6. Shoelaces, replacement spikes and tool.

7. Sunscreen.

8. One dozen of our best shag balls, a half dozen new balls. Three dozen tees.

9. At least one: Ball marker, divot repair tool, glove, cigar trimmer.

10. We usually pack one golf towel for every two rounds.

HAWK'S NEST GOLF CLUB

2800 East Pleasant Home Rd.
Creston
330.435.4611
www.Hawk'snest.osu.edu

THE WOOSTER INN

801 East Wayne Ave.
Wooster
330.263.2660
www.thewoosterinn.com

May we propose a toast? To Betty Hawkins, a Friend to Golf. To Mrs. Hawkins, whose love for golf and generosity to the game will be an enduring legacy.

Hear, hear! Bartender, more whiskey for my friends!

Mrs. Hawkins built **Hawk's Nest Golf Club**. Now you know from whence came the name. This self-effacing, determined woman enjoyed golf, especially her nine-hole ladies league.

In 1993, she had Hawk's Nest built. And more recently, she gave it away. Sort of. As she nears the Real Home Hole, she wanted to make sure her course would always be a golf course. So she gave it to *THE* Ohio State University's Agricultural Technical Institute. ATI produces golf course superintendents the way the University of Florida produces great football players.

Whoa, back it up a bit. The property Mrs. Hawkins placed in the hands of designer Steve Burns was formerly a farm. All 200 acres of it. Lots of the terrain is rolling, but some goes up and down at a more precipitous rate. He used all natural ingredients: the mature trees, the water, changes in elevation. There are holes on this course that made us think: Mother Nature wanted it this way. Burns found a way to accommodate Her. Few courses can brag about every hole being different. Hawk's Nest can and that's one of the unsung virtues of this course.

The first couple times we played it, we had two thoughts: first, that Steve Burns had a riot putting this course together, and second, there is a great deal of fun to be had here. Bent grass greens and blue grass fairways and rough, by the way.

Giving the course to ATI is not the only change. The nines have been flopped and it's one of those rare instances where the course plays better.

And faster. With the flop, the finishing holes—the ones you remember most easily—are built to shoot pars. Even better, No. 1 is now a par 5, the least resistant to par 5 on the course. What's better than a par or even a birdie on the first hole? The flop also mitigated what used to be an interminable wait on old No. 2 tee. The problem was/is a blind tee shot and players on the tee wait too long to lock, load and fire.

The original No. 7, now on the backside with a new name, continues to overpower players. The tee shot of this par 5 is blind and uphill and if length is not your strength, the second shot is blind as well. From the top of the hill, only a couple obstacles to the green, including a deep ravine and water. We played it as a par 7 and two of us were able to bogey.

Not every player is amenable to change. For example, one of the members in our group always suggests, when bets are being made, that we play the stymie rule.

Even before getting to the first tee, though, take a look at this driving range. And it's a public course, too. The majority of private clubs don't have driving ranges like this: like John Wayne used to ride in the saddle, high, wide, and handsome. Deep tee area, so it can be moved easily and we never warm up hitting off dirt.

On the course, it's wonderful conditioning. And, man, is it ever quiet. At the intersection of a state route and a county highway, the roads are not busy with eighteen-wheelers. Add to that electric carts and the only unnatural noises made are by men and their cries are either joyous or profane. No middle ground.

Hawk's Nest rarely toots its own horn, yet does a very good business. The best advertising is personal referral, and this place gets it.

The Wooster Inn is just a bit over 50 years old. Young in Sequoia Land, old in Ford Motor Land. The property is part of the College of Wooster. Seeing young men prance about in kilts is not unusual. The Fighting Scots gather here.

The Inn is neither big nor glitzy; it is classic, quiet, solid, comfortable. Here, it's not a pool room, but a billiards room. The emphasis is on quiet quality and slipping on a blazer for dinner is not overdressing.

Almost eight years ago, proprietor Ken Bogucki bought the place. He renovated eleven of the fifteen rooms, added a 3,000-square-foot patio, and poured $100,000 into the new Wooster Inn Pub, where we ate, drank and made merry.

In the warm weather, the chef has a happy hour on the patio. Do not be surprised to find yourself chatting with a guest who speaks fluent Russian and knows more about gulags than Solzhenitsyn—you're talking with a faculty member whose specialty is Russia. Or a comely coed who lectures you on Kant; philosophy is a major study here. Or a cheerleader. What the heck, more than 300 guests show up for delectable appetizers and cocktails.

If appetizers whet your appetite, dinner in the formal dining room can be an elegant touch to the getaway. The menu changes with the seasons, so you may not eat as we did: lobster bisque and pot stickers before baked walleye and chicken and mashed taters. We passed on salads. All the meals and dishes have the chef's unique touch, and the chicken is a good example. The stuffing is apple-cherry.

If you dine in the new pub, let us know how the Becca burger is. Before it's placed on the grill, it's stuffed with smoked Gouda and then, when the charred li'l baby comes off the grill, more cheese. Beer menu is equally tempting. Is a bottle of Smuttynose from New Hampshire

Hawk's Nest Golf Club

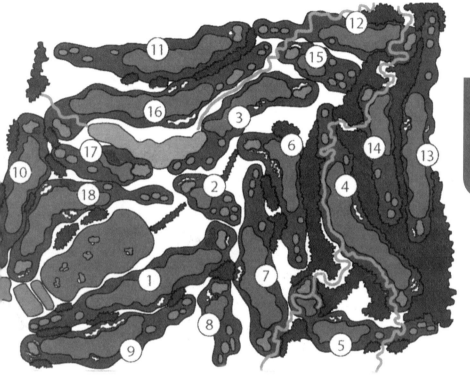

GOLF IN HINCKLEY, OHIO

Most of us who live south of Columbus know nothing of Hinckley, the little town jammed on the northern border of Medina County. More is the pity; this place has a golfer's six pack unlike any other. Five courses and a day set aside for welcoming migrating buzzards.

The buzzard thing? Every year, buzzards return to Hinckley. From where we don't know. But the town gets excited and somehow knows the exact day they will return. At least they say they do. And as your Aunt Louise counseled, when it comes down to fact or legend, always go with legend. Sounds like a great reason for a party.

But for our purposes, the carrion-eating monsters are second to golf in Hinckley. Five independent 18-hole courses: Ironwood, Skyland, Pine Hills, Hinckley Hills, and Valleaire. Ninety holes of golf, close enough to each other that you could strap your sticks to your Schwinn and pedal from one to another. From the white tees, it plays 30,470 yards and par is 359.

The oldest is Skyland, which was created in 1928. Me'ns suits were twenty bucks and included two pairs of pants. The wife of the second owner of the course believed she was the inspiration for the pull cart because she tossed

her sticks in a perambulator instead of carrying them. Drivers on State Route 303 had to see that.

The course with the most *Golf Digest* stars is Pine Hills, built in 1957 and home to the most dramatic finishing hole: a 420-yard par 4 dogleg left. The approach has to be airborne over a lake. Even better, everyone in the clubhouse or on the practice green has a great, unobstructed view).

Ironwood and Hinckley Hills are across the street from each other. Both feature severe changes in elevation and the finishing hole on the front side at Hinckley is 600 straightaway yards over a roller coaster fairway. Entire left side is out of bounds. Even the really good players have a challenge making par.

Valleaire was built by the Knights of Columbus, who were frustrated getting tee times for its traveling league. When Catholics want to play, they play.

SHALE CREEK GOLF CLUB

5420 Wolff Rd.

Medina

330.723.8774

www.shalecreekgolfclubggp.com

CAMBRIA SUITES

1787 Thorn Dr.

Uniontown

330.899.1990

www.cambriasuitesakron.com

Here's an unappreciated virtue for any hotel providing golf getaways: nearness to the interstate highway system. It makes getting there so easy. If one car in the caravan has to drop out for a pit stop, so what? The directions can be more clear than marching orders: Take I-77 (or I-480, or I-75, or I-71) to an exit number, get off and look around.

So it is with **Cambria Suites** in Uniontown; if you can find I-77, you can find the Cambria. Not to sound like the p.r. guy for the hotel, but this new (four years old) hostelry, hard by the highway, does so much right that nitpickers are frustrated. The economy has slowed Cambria growth, but it has eighteen hotels. The first one in Boise, Idaho.

Cambria is too new to have much experience with golf getaways. (Or the PGA Tour, but once Tour players stayed here, they came back. It's a quick shot to Firestone.) Once the dust settled, Mike Lorenzo, the revenue and front office manager, volunteered to service the market. He knows first-hand the joys of getaways, and first sat down to make notes about his own experiences. He looked at it from three perspectives: as a hotel manager, as a member of the guys, and as The Guy.

As a member of the guys, he wanted cold beer and good food. Substandard food can destroy a getaway faster than a thunderstorm.

While good meals, like high scores, are quickly forgotten, no one forgets a bad dining experience. Or any digestive distress. It becomes part of the getaway lore. Next on his list was a combination: comfort and value. The guys don't want to gossip about thin towels or a cranky air conditioning unit. Most of us are Midwesterners, so good value for a good buck makes sense. Next was perfect coordination between hotel and courses.

Pretty short and reasonable list.

The list for The Guy, however, was more detailed and more important. The Guy is responsible for the foundations of the getaway and if all the stanchions aren't secure, only disaster can result.

Lorenzo found that when looking at The Guy's work, there was no listing his responsibilities in any particular order. Each was vital. The Guy selected a course or courses, a hotel, found out how many members would be going, collected deposits, made the tee times, printed up driving directions, made arrangements with the hotel, and put together foursomes based on handicaps.

When it works well, members of the group thank The Guy. Smarter members profusely thank The Guy, and silently pray he will do it again next year.

Mike Lorenzo, meet Robert D'Agostino.

D'Agostino is a Toledo police officer and The Guy for a twenty-eight-man platoon of cops on getaway. (Somehow it feels odd writing about cops and their getaways. Is there a sitcom here? Maybe, "Cops on Getaways?") He has been The Guy for a long time and knows more about golf getaways in the Midwest than almost anyone.

Now, most getaways are fewer than twenty-eight guys, so D'Agostino's workload is increased by number of deposits sent, tee times, figuring who would play best with each other, etc., etc., etc. In his group, handicaps range from 5 to 22.

D'Agostino's group was at the Cambria for four nights and five days of golf. After explaining his experience throughout the Midwest as The Guy, he was asked to describe the experience at Cambria. He said only three words: "Great. The best." Hmm. High praise from The Guy.

One of the reasons is Cambria's connection with courses. Two new courses, The Quarry and Shale Creek Golf Club, make a great one-two punch in Ohio golf. That would be enough for any reasonable getaway. More than enough, actually. But Cambria created partnerships with three private clubs: Medina CC, Prestwick CC and Rosemont CC.

The other reason, of course, was Cambria. All the details The Guy needed were covered. The courses, tee times and explicit directions. When two guys, such as D'Agostino and Lorenzo get together, it is like Laurel and Hardy: great stuff and perfect timing.

D'Agostino once had his getaway gang registering at the desk when one cop asked another, "Do you have your gun?" The other cop said, "No, I left it in the car." A civilian couple, also in line to register, promptly walked out, never to be seen again.

The rooms are spacious with high ceilings, the carpeting Stimps at 8.5, the beds are the most comfortable since we left the bassinet. *Wall Street Journal* is delivered daily. Televisions are hanging on walls, taking the place of bad hotel artwork.

The hotel is modern design, though it would take an architectural student to accurately name the style. We called it Handsome Modern, but don't expect that designation to be accepted. Most distinguishing is the space. Everything is here, but nothing gets in the way. It is very quiet at night. All rooms here are suites, so poker is comfortable. We pulled the desktop (on wheels) in front of the couch and put chairs on the other side. Refrigerator is close by. The men's room is, well, it's modern and different. Functional as all get out, but not one to show the wife, lest she decides she wants one just like it, and suddenly, the golf outing has a $20,000 remodeling bill attached.

Remember when the hotel soap was two, tiny bars from an unknown manufacturer? Cambria's bathroom is stocked with (we're not kidding): coconut lime verbena, a shower gel; Pleasures, a coconut lime verbena, a volumizing conditioner (for the guy who still does comb-overs?); a warm-vanilla-sugar-rich cleansing bar infused with real vanilla extract and another infused with real coconut extract. Word to the wise: If you're an Ivory guy, pack your own soap.

The dining at Cambria is a balance between business casual and ease of dining. The fulcrum is quality. We walked out the back of the hotel to enjoy a smoke en route to the dining room (dining room, bar, front desk, lounge have no doors between them, are easily navigated and all have televisions hanging on the walls). The chef had walked out, too, to enjoy a smoke. So we chatted about food service until we asked for recommendations. Chef Debbie Schwab (no relation to Charles) suggested the lemon-pepper chicken with artichokes for one of us and the hamburger for the other.

Not easy finding a high-quality, savory hamburger. When we went to our table, Debbie had already started our meals. Both were excellent. The hamburger was made of high grade beef, perfectly cooked and so good it needed absolutely nothing: no condiments, no tomato slice, no nothing. The chicken was equally good. Tender meat, lots and lots of pasta with a creamy sauce and plenty of artichokes.

Two minor points about Cambria. When we were there, we noticed license plates in the parking lot. In addition to Ohio, there were plates from Indiana, New York, Pennsylvania, Oklahoma, New Hampshire, South Carolina and Florida. Make of it what you will.

Second, there is in the parking lot a nice GMC van, decorated with Cambria all over it. It is used to pick up guests at nearby Akron-Canton Airport, but if you need it, just ask. Didn't pack enough smokes? Forgot your 56-degree wedge in the shower? Need socks or a belt? Drink a bit much and worried about getting back to the hotel? If the van is there, it and a driver are yours. Just ask.

We played **Shale Creek Golf Club** and were impressed throughout the round, which began with a trip to the driving range. Target greens, silos in the distance, an employee constantly refilling the ball buckets. At the starter's post, the starter fished bottles of ice cold water for the twosome and added cheese and peanut sandwiches, along with best wishes for a fun round. It doesn't start any better than that.

Five tees here, the gold is the longest at 7,026 yards, and the green markers play 5,043 yards. We played the whites, 5,913 yards. Most of the front side is open, which means subject to the whims of wind. Even without trees, the closely-mowed fairways point the way and leaving the fairway to challenge blue grass rough is a no-win situation. Some players find open courses more challenging than parkland because of the wind and the rough.

General Manager Brad Cavey is especially proud of the architect, Brian Huntley, who worked for many years with Arthur Hills. The clubhouse is a temporary structure and as the economy rebounds, a real one will be built. In the meantime, the pro shop here does just fine.

While the course is part of a housing development, the housing doesn't get in the way; neither is it a distraction.

There is "sneaky water" here, ponds and some streams that first-timers don't see until they're in them. This hazard that can be avoided using the GPS. For all the openness of the front side, the back side demands a bit more accuracy.

The back side tightens up considerably and the course suddenly goes from wide open to target golf. The course winds through new housing and crosses a couple roads, but the housing doesn't get close enough to become a hazard. Speaking of hazards, designer Brian Huntley is excellent with bunkering. Some are optical illusions, all are perfectly maintained, and a sandy on any hole is a source of pride. Finishing holes 17 and 18 remind us how important stamina is to golf. Seventeen is a long par 3 followed by a long par 4. Our tees were 142 yards and 363 yards, but the waybacks are 209 yards and 461 yards.

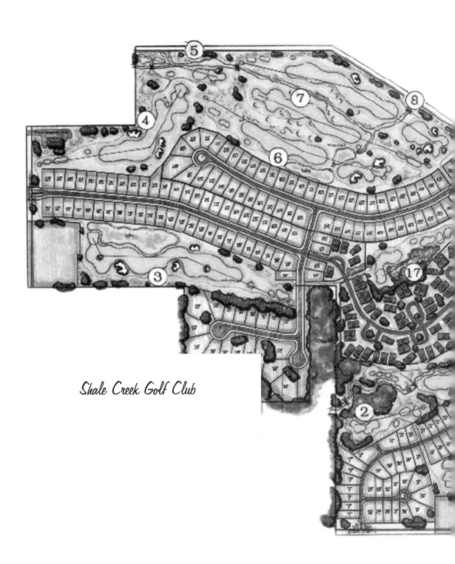

Shale Creek Golf Club

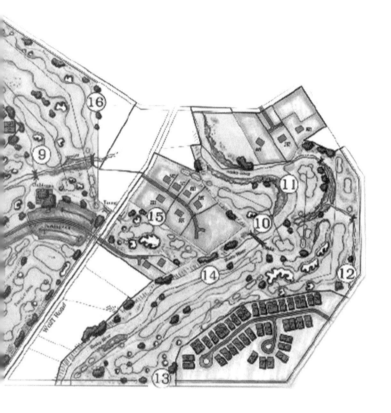

CHIPPEWA GOLF COURSE

12147 Shank Rd.
Doylestown
330.658.6126
www.chippewagolfclub.com

BARBERTON BROOKSIDE COUNTRY CLUB

3727 Golf Course Rd.
Barberton
330.825.4538
www.barbertonbrookside.com

HOLIDAY INN AKRON AND HYDE PARK GRILLE

4073 Medina Rd.
Akron
330.666.4131

DEVORE'S HOPOCAN GARDENS

4396 Hopocan Ave.
Barberton
330.825.9923
www.hopocangardens.com

Ever go on a getaway where the food was first and the golf was second? Us, neither, but between the food and the golf in Barberton, we could understand it if you did.

Man Food served here. Great steaks at one place and at another, arguably the best thing that ever happened to a chicken.

The Holiday Inn on I-77 and State Route 18, just a bit west of Akron, was command central. Here are the good things about this Holiday Inn:

1. No one is going to get lost getting there. If you can find I-77, you can find the hotel.
2. It's a Holiday Inn. No surprises. Professional staff has been

doing it a long time. Remember, they compete for our dollars with eagerness not seen since Hertz and Avis stepped into the ring.

3. A $2 million renovation just finished. So don't spill anything. Big lobby with waterfall and fireplace.

4. Three suites. To facilitate the timely playing of poker, there are two bathrooms in each suite. Trés elegant.

5. They're used to us. They've seen plenty of golfers walking out, early morning, with bleary eyes and bed head, determined to make that tee time. Unless your credit card is declined, it means nothing to them.

6. Hyde Park Grille and Montrose Bar and Grill. All the cooking is done by Hyde Park. The steak at Hyde Park is an event; the lunch and dinner at the Montrose is casual and very good.

7. The bar. This is hardly a shot and a beer joint. You're blessed if the regular bartender, Shawn Daugherty, is there. He's the author of, *Extra Dry, with a Twist: An Insider's Guide to Bartending*, available on Amazon or right across the bar.

Enough already; let's go tee it up. **Barberton Brookside Country Club** is one of golf's granddaddies. Laid out in 1921, when Ohio boy Warren G. Harding was president of the United States.

The course isn't long and isn't penal. Bent grass on small greens, blue grass other places. The course gently rises and falls, and with a minimum of water and sand bunkers, it is far less hazardous than say, cleaning your gutters.

It is pure fun. Both sides start with long par 5s (581 and 535) and while they're not long, getting on in regulation calls for accurate iron play. The small greens can be deceptive, and the winner, at day's end, will likely be the guy with the great short game. (How many times do we have to hear that?)

We don't know about the fauna, but the flora adds to the course, both at the tee boxes and bordering fairways. Give us a day in June, a tee time here, a beautiful woman—and you can keep the beautiful woman.

An additional pleasure is knowing the course we're on is the same course played by generation after generation of aficionados. When the dedication round was played in the early '20s, a major technological advance was getting underway: the tee. Here's a little history for you: the tee, which was designed to replace mounds of dirt made by the players, was designed and patented in 1899. And the guy who did it was an African-American dentist in Boston, Dr. George Franklin Grant. He didn't do much with it, though, and when he died, in 1910, the tee went with him.

Fast forward a dozen years and another dentist (geez—do these guys ever work?), Dr. William Lowell, fashioned wooden tees from white birch and had the great Walter Hagen use them. Sold like hotcakes, made a lot of money, tempted all sorts of imitators and Dr. Lowell spent lots of money in court, charging patent infringement.

Give us a day in June, a tee time here, a beautiful woman—and you can keep the beautiful woman.

Not long after the wooden tee made the game easier, **DeVore's Hopocan Gardens** opened on Hopocan Avenue. Not to belabor the history part of this getaway, but Hopocan was an Indian chief who lived in the area. When the joint opened in the '30s, it was more bar and beer garden than restaurant. That was more than seventy years ago and its development, without benefit of restaurant consultants, is worthy of a book. Very short book, but still, the place is an important part of Barberton history as well as Barberton today.

Hopocan's (accent is on the first syllable) is one of Barberton's famous chicken houses, and the third generation is getting ready to pass ownership on to the fourth. There are others, such as Whitehouse, and Belgrade Gardens among them. Paprika spoken here.

Let's just say a monsoon has pretty much closed the course. Our suggestion is a late lunch and then a late dinner. Yes, both at Hopocan's. On Tuesdays, and Tuesdays only, stuffed cabbage is prepared by hand, using a family recipe older than wooden tees.

And for dinner? Hopocan's chicken. None of this doctored-ordered poached chicken breast on a bed of greens and low calorie dressing. The place brags that its chicken is fried in lard. No trans fats. If you want to know the many pleasures of lard, ask your Aunt Louise. (Be careful how you phrase the question.) Her mom cooked with the stuff every day and the reason her pie crusts were the envy of the neighborhood was—lard. You can get other stuff here, but if you pass on the fried chicken and hot rice, you've got a screw loose. Rice? Yeah, rice. The dish started out as a tangy dipping sauce and today is mixed with rice. Just as the chicken is special to Barberton, so is this side dish that went from hot sauce to hot rice. The bar serves beer and wine only. As if you needed anything else.

Whoops—we're here to play golf, too, so let the belt out two notches and let's tee it up. **Chippewa Golf Course** is another course that isn't long, around 6,500 yards at its longest, but revered among the locals. Management brags that the course has its own Amen Corner. After going through it a couple times, we think Novena Corner would be more accurate. But that was then and this is now.

This year it isn't the course on which former owner Billy Brown, Sr., shot a record 64. Mr. Brown is now 84 and still plays.

Anyway, last year, major improvements were made and they included adding a couple ponds, a mess of new fairway bunkers, and the reconfiguring of a number of holes: No. 1 is now a par 5; the par 3 at No. 14 has been reconfigured; No. 15 is now a par 3. Par is now 72 instead of 71. The greens have always been bent and Kentucky blue in the fairways and rough. Changes are on a par with Lincoln Town Cars, 1989 to 1990.

But that's not the challenging part here. It's the big, sweet, curvy greens. You think the haircut you got at boot camp was short? These babies are slicker than snot on a door handle. These are the greens on which guys comment on their putts, "Except for direction and distance, that would have been a good putt." For scoring purposes, the best part of the season is aeration time. Then, no matter how unskilled with the putter, we can say, "Take two and pick it up."

Management here is happy to see you. If you play your first round before heading off to Hopocan's, you can get directions in the pro shop. Don't be foolish; go hungry.

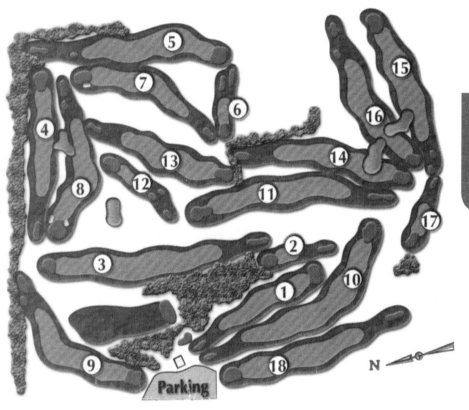

Chippewa Golf Course

N

Parking

HOW TO BALL HAWK

The late Charley Stone was the head pro at Beechmont Country Club, in Cleveland. His pro shop had every brand and type of ball except crystal. He was once asked, "What's the best ball?" His answer: "The one I have the most of."

He went on to say that for many players, it doesn't matter whether we're hitting a two-piece, three-piece or any of the hybrids. While balls can be engineered to perform in pretty specific ways, those balls are engineered for very good players.

For guys with terminal slices, or duck hooks, golf suddenly becomes an expensive proposition.

Enter ball hawking, the ancient skill of finding lost balls in the woods, under water, or deep rough.

The benefits of ball hawking are legion:

1. Gives you a chance to be at the course without raising your handicap;
2. You get to wear your baseball cap backwards without looking like a moron. (You don't want the cap being pulled off by branches. More on dressing for hawking later.);
3. You meet such interesting animals in the woods;
4. If you're middle-class, finding a ball is like finding a fifty-cent piece. A joy!;
5. You never have to buy balls again. What ball do you prefer to play? Nike? Srixon? They're in there, waiting for you;
6. Hawking stretches your hamstrings, sharpens your ability to focus and reminds you how important your sense of direction is (not for hawking, but getting back out of the woods).

The essence of ball hawking, like many other endeavors, is focus. Remember, you're looking for a small, white ball weighing only 1.62 ounces and measuring only 1.68 inches in diameter. Sounds simple, but until somebody told me, I was a double bogey hawker. Today I'm always in the red numbers. Timing is vital, too.

The best hawking is done following the last group of any league or outing. And for the same reasons. Most leagues, as you know, are filled with men who love to play and shoot the breeze. But it's clear golf is not the way they put food on the table. Outings are the same except the players tend to drink more. Anyway, my point is this: When these guys duck hook a Titleist or seriously slice a Top Flite, they have neither time nor incentive to tromp through the woods, looking for the errant ball.

When you find a brand new Pro V, and then another one within ten yards, you can assume the guy at the tee hit first one, then the second one, both badly, then finally said, "Oh, I'm gonna drop it out there." His loss, your gain. I say "his" because women rarely lose balls. First of all, they don't hit it as far and second, they hit it straighter. End of story.

You want to dress for the occasion. Just as you would wear clodhoppers and bib overalls to plow the back forty, a trip into the woods calls for long pants (no sense rubbing up against poison ivy), golf shoes, (as your therapist said, "get a grip!") a baseball cap and shirt of your choice (I like a long-sleeved tee shirt). Equipment? Some balls are on the other side of heavy brush, so I always take a sand wedge with me. For me, it's the best use of that club. An empty shag bag is often a good idea. Reappearing from the bush with two dozen balls in your pockets is unattractive and uncomfortable. A good dousing with insect repellent will keep the deer flies from feasting on you.

My ol' pal Jerry McGinty, a former caddy, said to comb the area just within the wood line. Ah, Jer, technology passed you by! With graphite shafts, driver heads the size of wheel blocks, and balls so ready to go long that their engines are revving before we address them—the heck with the wood line. The balls are in the deep woods. (Another reason to pay attention to direction. After loading up, you want to get out without the assistance of rescue dogs. We know from literature the futility of dropping bread crumbs behind us.)

'Kay, dressed for it? Lots of bug juice on? Shoes securely tied? Sand wedge at the ready? Empty shag bag in your hip pocket? Cap on backwards? Let's go!

Because you're focused on small, white balls, you might not pay attention to branches. Don't worry. You'll pay attention after you get your face slapped a few times.

You'll see your first ball within a few minutes. Do not get all excited. It's the first of many. As you pick it up and marvel at the brand name, look around. If one duffer could put one there, so can others. Your focus will become sharper and you'll spot the white of a golf ball even if most of the ball is hidden under leaves or sticks. Visually scout a small area you want to cover, and then go over it carefully. Then another small area, and another, and another. (This is a great time to enjoy smoking without everyone complaining about you and smoke is a natural bug repellent.)

Balls obey the law of gravity as well as anything else, but they tend to get hung up on fallen trees and bushes, so go slowly there and reap the benefits. There is no rush in hawking.

You can stay until dark, though I limit my forays to the time it takes to enjoy one cigar. Depending on the amount of league play and outings since I've last been there, I usually bring a couple dozen balls out and there are only two or three bad ones.

Do not tell anyone where your "honey hole" is. None of their business. Take the balls home, wash them with dishwashing soap, dry them and put them back in your shag bag.

Now you have enough practice balls to cure that slice or unbend that hook. Use them—you don't want to be a supplier to Hawk's like me.

THE QUARRY GOLF CLUB

5650 Quarry Lake Dr.
Canton
330.488.3178
www.quarrygolfclubggp.com

HOLIDAY INN HOTEL
(BELDEN VILLAGE)

4520 Everhard Rd. NW
North Canton
330.494.2770

If you take a cell phone with you when teeing it up at **The Quarry Golf Club**, you have no respect for golf. To enjoy this new course (as well as Mother Nature,) all you need is a decent swing, a trusty putter, and a good cigar.

We've always liked Canton because the Pro Football Hall of Fame is there, and Bender's Restaurant, too. Any restaurant that can make it more than a century (and sell turtle soup for more than a half century) is our kind of town. When we put Bender's and The Quarry in the same sentence, it's like introducing a hall of famer to the first round draft pick. And we add: To drink where Jim Thorpe drank.

With its growing golf riches, perhaps the Big Three—Cleveland, Columbus, and Cincinnati—will become the Big Four: Canton for golf, Columbus for insurance and government, Cincinnati for Pete Rose, and Cleveland for the Rock and Roll Hall of Fame.

The Quarry has what has been referred to as a sister club, Shale Creek, in York Township. Having these two gems is like having Venus and Serena Williams in your neighborhood. Both are by Granite Golf Management. The courses, not the sisters.

Both courses were designed by Brian Huntley and this is just a guess, but after playing a number of Huntley courses, we think no designer has more fun at work than this talented guy from Unionville.

Some of the features even before you agree on the bets: driving range, practice green, and a chipping green. Might be a good idea to get there early, just to enjoy the clubhouse, which sits at the end of the quarry lake and has great views of finishing holes. The Granite Grill is here, too, and leaving without spending some time here is difficult.

When Huntley first looked at a topo map of the property, he knew the holes were there. The challenge was deciding which hole went where: what terrain would provide a good opening hole, which hills and valleys would fit a par 5, the role water would play, where the par 3s would be both beautiful and playable. The late, great Ohio amateur champ Edwin Preisler used to say that when he stepped on to a par 3 tee box, he wanted three things from the design. First, he wanted the hole to be beautiful. Second, he wanted it to be well-defined. Third, he wanted the hole to make him stop and think before selecting a club.

Every hole on this young course is worthy of being on a postcard.

On a property that had been quarried for decades, Huntley was looking at lots of water, great changes in elevation, and enough stands of mature timber to excite any tree hugger. But here's the unwritten part of the designer's contract: You only get one chance to route it right. (And don't get us started on the design of some Ohio courses that leave much to be desired.)

It all begins at the clubhouse, a 23,000 square foot palace with lovely landscaping. Add a "hop-to-it" staff, practice facilities, and a starter who really likes his job. State-of-the-art GPS. Everything after that, of course, is on your shoulders.

It is very much a thinking player's course and unrealistic to think you'll shoot your best the first few rounds. That's another virtue of the Quarry; lots of memorable holes that you just know you can play better. Maybe next time a 5-iron instead of a 6-iron to get up to that green, maybe a 3-wood off the tee instead of the driver, maybe paying more attention to dat o' debbil wind. The list can go on and on, which is one of Quarry's pleasures.

Remember the old line about having one's ball retriever regripped? The water here is deep; leave the retriever in the trunk. As he does with bunkering, Huntley does with water; it isn't there to snatch balls, but to make the course beautiful, define the holes and if you make a really bad shot, only then to take it away from you. Fescue and steep-lipped pot bunkers add great color.

Every hole on this young course is worthy of being on a postcard, and especially the tee at No. 17, from which you see downtown Canton and wonder aloud, "How the heck did they drop a golf course in here?" From the tips, it plays 7,015 yards (course rating is 74, slope is 139); from the whites, 6,004 yards (69/125), and front or forwards, 4,878 yards (68.4/117). There are five tees and if you make the mistake of selecting the wrong tee box, you're not going to enjoy yourself. One of the features of modern design is giving all tees the same care. It used to be the blues represented the designer's vision, the whites were put in for the ham-and-eggers, and the so-called "ladies tee" was an afterthought.

Not that anyone asked us, but we think a par 5 is the best way to begin a round. Here the round begins at an elevated tee with views enough to slow play. To look at the course from this vantage point is another way to enjoy the beauty of the woods and water. Five hundred twelve yards from our blue tees. The landing area is more generous that it appears from the tee, so if the draw or fade is a little reluctant (or overreaching), not to worry.

Given the terrain, no surprise that dogleg is spoken here, and a few look like ninety degrees. Hole Nos. 4 and 14 can be satisfying or confounding. Each is a short par 4, No. 4 only 282 yards and whether you go for it or not, you'll at least think about being a hero. Heroes here often get stuck in the bunker that protects the green. A fairway wood or long iron off the tee provides for a short iron approach. No. 14 is way different: a little longer at 314 yards and the eye-catching feature is a huge, flat boulder in the middle of the fairway. Bunkering, by the way, is gorgeous; not meant to be penal, but to keep players on the straight and narrow and to define holes. Or, in the case of the No. 4 tee, to challenge with an "are you man enough?" Few of us are. No. 15, a par 5 of 507 yards, is memorable, no matter your score: Drive a gorge and descend 150 feet, then play back up to a small green.

And be on your best behavior while you're there. One getaway player was thrown off the course for taking a leak in the woods. Now *that* caused some tension between club and hotel. We don't know, but our best guess is that the player wasn't as discreet as he might have been. In addition to the golf course, there is substantial residential development here. We stayed at the **Holiday Inn Hotel (Belden Village)**, which has been providing getaways for a couple decades. The largest getaway there was 200 guys, all with Teamster membership cards in their wallets. The hotel's best marketing success is Pittsburgh, a good example of how to draw out-of-state money here.

One group has been coming here since the packages were offered. Maybe the package agreed with The Guy because the hotel calls and confirms everything. Your tee time has your name on it and that cart over there, sir, is yours. Opening the Quarry, by the way, created an uptick with the hotel.

No shortage of area restaurants (though none with the creaking, affectionate history of Bender's), but we ate only at Bender's and the hotel. The chef at the hotel understands us. His golf season specials are along the lines of prime rib, barbecued ribs, and strip steaks.

Tam O'Shanter Golf Course

5055 Hills and Dales Rd. NW
Canton
330.477.5111
www.tamoshantergolf.com

Holiday Inn

4520 Everhard Rd. NW
Canton
330.494.2770

We like Canton. Always have. Its downtown Central Plaza is a knockout and lesson for urban planners; the NFL Hall of Fame is here, if you want to know what it was like when *real men* played the game; there is so much good golf in the area that we're thinking about retiring here.

Plus, when Canton, China, changed its name to Guangzhou, Canton, Ohio stayed the same. Whew.

Our first trip to Canton had nothing to do with golf; as kids, we came to the President William McKinley Presidential Library. He was reared and educated in Ohio, a brave and honored fighter in the Civil War, and given his work on behalf of unions, he should be St. William McKinley, Patron Saint of the Picket Line. But those are stories for another trip.

We stayed at the **Holiday Inn**, Belden Village. Good timing. In addition to the new logo, the hotel was recently renovated. Now those were some firm mattresses with crisp sheets. Microwave and refrigerator are among the amenities in every room.

A failure to spring for a suite for The Guy constitutes an

irreparable slight. Plus, it's the suite that has a parlor room (read: poker room), wet bar (read: we thought we died and went to heaven), conference table (read: poker table), new furniture and an extra half bath. We're in high cotton, I tell you. High cotton.

We packed our swim trunks. Good idea. Nice outdoor pool there. Played Tam O'Shanter two days in a row. First day: play golf, out to dinner, shower and put on the trunks. We don't swim; it's more like we lounge in the pool, sort of like manatees.

Love that breakfast buffet. Not to sound like critics, but we found the staff to be conscientious, friendly, and professional. It has always been our contention—and no wants want to argue—that the men and women in the hospitality business work harder than just about everybody else. Let's face it, there are customers out there who should be locked in the trunks of their cars, instead of being given room keys. Plus, the hours are long.

That's why we leave a tip for the housekeeper.

Not that we're hotel experts, but here, we think a good idea might be to make a dartboard with all the area restaurants. Slowed by an inability to make a decision? Just toss a dart and off you go. There are that many eateries and they're all pretty darn good. Close by, too. Designated driver is *de rigueur*.

And **Tam O'Shanter Golf Course**? One of Canton's brightest lights, as far as we're concerned. Excellent practice facilities. Two very good courses, one big and stately clubhouse with six columns in front and three gables on the roof, and the four of us. Two of the guys had not played here, so on both days we played two-man scrambles, a great way to be introduced to a golf course.

The courses are Hills and Dales. Little different from each other, but both well manicured. They served as home to the Ohio Open. And Hills and Dales describes the terrain. At one point, high on a hill, one of us asked how developers were able to drop two golf courses in a densely developed area. Well, truth is, the property was banked when the economy looked poorly on developers. That was more than 300 acres and two courses. Dales came to life in the late '20s, its fraternal twin in 1931. The commercial side of Canton grew up around the courses, which were there first.

There is a reason the Hills course is named Hills. From the back of the box, Hills plays 6,363 yards. Slope is 115 and course rating is 69.4. No. 6, a short par 4, is a good example. From the tee, it's straight uphill. Pretty hole, lined with trees, and accented with goldenrod and Queen Anne's Lace. The next hole is straight downhill, a par 4 dogleg that curls left. By now we're wondering why we brought the drivers with us.

No. 9 is another uphill, but it's a par 3. According to the scorecard, it plays 190 yards. According to us, it plays two and a half clubs longer. No. 13, most resistant to par on the back side, is over 400 yards, but that's not the tough part. The green has more tiers—three — than your birthday cake.

Careful when you get your cart. All are made by Yamaha, but the newer models don't have shock absorbers and by the end of the round, your kidney stones will have passed along with some other parts.

The Dales course plays 6,538 yards, with a 110 slope and 70.4 rating. It's par 70. Designed by Leonard Macomber, who prepped with Donald Ross, it was built in 1928. It's flatter than its fraternal twin, but no less fun. Just like the Hills, the ability to hit sidehill, downhill, and uphill lies is vital. So is putting. Wonderful greens whose speed matched the practice green. We hope it wasn't just dumb luck, but on both, play went fast.

Many Ohio golf professionals and competitive amateurs remember Edwin Preisler, the great amateur who passed away a few years ago. Take a look at the wizened old player who serves as Tammy's patron saint. If Eddie didn't pose for that, he had a twin. Even to wearing the tam.

Oak Shadows Golf Club

1063 Oak Shadows Dr. NE
New Philadelphia
330.343.2426
www.oakshadowsgolf.com

Whispering Pines B & B

1268 Magnolia Rd. (St. Rt. 542)
Dellroy (Atwood Lake)
330.735.2824
www.atwoodlake.com

Lighthouse Bistro

9800 Atwood Lake Rd.
Mineral City
330.343.0112
www.lighthousebistro.net

Every so often, man inadvertently stumbles across something of great and lasting value. It was an accident that allowed Charles Goodyear to discover the vulcanizing process. Same with Alexander Fleming and penicillin.

So it is with the many journeys taken for this book. We sought golf getaways for guys, not a complicated or challenging assignment when you think about it. Even enviable to listen to some.

Appearances are so deceiving. Leona Helmsley looked pretty sweet and Eldrick Woods made us think he was the model of virtue. So it goes.   ·

We were just taking the slow route home from Atwood Lake when we found **Whispering Pines Bed and Breakfast**. Big and handsome farmhouse, the sort of place young couples go for their first wedding anniversary or the Ladies Sewing Guild books for its summer getaway.

And what did we discover? We found Whispering Pines to be the ultimate for a golf getaway. A few years ago, The Guy wouldn't be calling bed and breakfast places to arrange golf getaways, especially because the two were never used in the same sentence.

That was then; this is now.

At the Pines, we found food and comfort and personal service unavailable at hotels. Here's the surprise: They like us. They really like us.

What's your pleasure? Seven card stud? Five card draw? Texas Hold 'Em? Right this way, gentlemen, to the card room. And what a card room. The antique furnishings had us wishing we would have dressed in our Bret and Bart Maverick clothes.

What's your pleasure? Nine ball? Straight? Slop? Rack 'em up and chalk that cue, sir. (Actually, the pool table is not in yet, but it will be soon.)

When the sun went down, we sat around a fire pit in the backyard. Every star in the Milky Way was shining bright. The roaring fire pit was as conducive to conversation as an AA meeting. Want popcorn? You got it.

You say you shoot? What do you say before we hit the road for home tomorrow, we get in some practice. Part of the package can be a range with three courses (two 50-bird and one 100-bird, and a catwalk.) Didn't pack the ol' 12-gauge? (It's not on anyone's check-off list when they pack.) Not to worry; they have guns and shells there.

If the coffee were any fresher, Juan Valdez would be unloading his donkey in the backyard.

Feel like fishing? See that little boat over there? Atwood Lake and that boat are all yours. Catch and release, will you? Innkeeper Linda Horn has many talents, but cleaning fish isn't one of them.

When we return this season, we'll plan a little better. First, a late morning or early afternoon tee time at Oak Shadows. Second, pack our Bret and Bart Maverick clothes. Third, if we can find the Pocket Fisherman, it goes in the bag, right next to the L.L. Bean shooting glasses.

Breakfast is served from 9 to 10:30 in the morning, which struck us as the most civilized time for Linda Horn's freshbaked breads and sliced in-season fruits, and eggs in myriad guises. When was the last time you had lemon ricotta pancakes? Lots of juices and if the coffee were any fresher, Juan Valdez would be unloading his donkey in the backyard.

Bill and Linda Horn are from Michigan, a station in life that should not be held against them. They have been Buckeyes for more than twenty years, and their story is worth telling.

They were picking up an antique bookcase in the Atwood Lake area, and before leaving, moseyed down Route 542. Up on a hill was the farmhouse and they pulled in to look. The view from the farmhouse, hard by Atwood Lake, was nothing short of spectacular. When they were admiring the house and the view and the property, they decided it would be a great B & B, unmindful of the fact that neither had any experience as an innkeeper.

They called the owner and asked if the property was for sale. When the owner said yes, the Horns said, we'll buy it. Oh, and by the way, they added, how much? This was before, mind you, they had been inside. They bought it for the views and the farmhouse would come along with them.

The farmhouse was built in 1880, and is in better shape today than it was then; Bill's toolbox has just about every tool known to Western man and he knows how to use them. (If you get a chance, ask him about some of his projects. We did and he made each of us feel like slackers.)

Just as The Guy is a natural for golf getaways, the Horns are naturals to inn keeping. Over the years, the kitchen was redone (wait till you see the huge Viking commercial stove), rooms renovated and furnished with antiques, an old porch torn off and replaced with a sun room, flowers and waterfalls put in and tended, wiring and plumbing brought up to code, and Bill has lots more plans for this summer. They did nothing at all with the views, leaving that to Mother Nature.

Linda recommended supper at the **Lighthouse Bistro**, just our kind of place. It's on the lake, has some outdoor dining, and serves whitefish. Boring name for that bug-eyed creature but we first enjoyed it in Michigan, where it must be the state fish, and here, this firm and tasty morsel is beer battered. Along with it, garlic mashed potatoes. Also enjoyed a huge Great Lake Dortmunder from the tap and a couple more of us had Guinness. There are some beers here that we didn't try, but will: Negro Modela and Blue Moon among them. One at the table had only appetizers and walked out filled: the mussels, he said, were magnificent and the bruschetta was memorable. A review couldn't be any better or any more succinct.

Oak Shadows Golf Club is twenty minutes away and there are closer places to stay. None better, just closer. As we did with a number of getaways, we went first to the course and played and then to our lodging and out for supper. The next day, we played a second time and then hit the road for home. That is a good example of getting all the golf you can from a trip. Always ask about the replay fee at courses. You might end up playing thrity-six the first day and thirty-six the second. Seventy-two holes on an overnighter sates the passion madmen have for golf.

Before it was a knockout golf course, the property here was used for other purposes, notably strip mining, hunting and off-road vehicles, the bane of baby rabbits. No evidence remains.

Plenty of changes in elevation, lots of water, and the physical beauty of course. Tee positions so it can play as long as 7,000 yards and as short as 5,200 yards. It's no secret we like to start play with a leisurely par 5, and this opening hole is 573 yards from the blues, but anything but leisurely. It's serpentine, demands accuracy for every shot (especially the tee shot), and wastes no time bringing sand and water into play.

Love the tees on No. 5, separate and elevated they are, and this par 3 is 171 yards, with sand front left and water right and back. Club selection is vital, of course, just as vital as a smooth swing. Failure with either one means trouble.

Have to love No. 7, a long par 4 with water front and back. Good thing is the water is largely psychological. That means that it won't come into play unless you really screw up and if you do, you'll go crazy.

The back side is as glorious as the front. No. 11 is a par 5, a mere 503 yards, but (there's always a "but," isn't there?) players have to carry water to get to the fairway.

Home hole is tempting. Everything you have to do is clearly in front and with a good drive, the green on this 511-yard par 5 suddenly looks reachable. However (there's always a "however," too, isn't there?) the green is protected first by water and then by sand. Geez, what else could they add? Pricker bushes? But getting on in regulation means par and sometimes better.

Oak Shadows Golf Club

Clubhouse

Parking

Driving
Range

SALT FORK STATE PARK

14755 Cadiz Rd.
Lore City
740.439.3521
www.saltforkstatepark.com

Look, the state park at **Salt Fork State Park** is almost 18,000 acres. The heck with the GPS on your cart; keep one dangling around your neck. Especially during hunting season. No sense having The Guy explain to your survivors that you went into the woods, looking for an errant drive, only to be mistaken for a ruffed grouse.

Golf is open year 'round, weather permitting.

It's a family place, so if the thought of chattering, running, jumping kids reminds you too much of reform school, the park has a wealth of cottages. Have to say, however, the kids we saw were pretty nice kids, well-mannered and clearly enjoying themselves.

On our way to the registration desk, we came across a pumpkin carver. His pumpkin weighed 1,274 pounds and looked like it. We brought home a single seed that will be planted in a week or two. More as it develops.

Big-beamed structure and equally big windows throughout, the design is simple and handsome; lots of heavy, wooden furniture, including rockers, leather couches and easy chairs.

The lodge has 148 guest rooms, but more important, thirty-seven cottages, each a two-bedroom and all having full kitchens. Best of all, screened porches, so while the mosquitoes sing the song of the frustrated, we were able to play poker without knocking over the stack of chips or slapping ourselves. And here's a pleasant note; dogs are permitted. Probably other types of pets, too, but golfers tend to be lovers of dogs. We didn't bring Ol' Roy, and have no plans to, but it's nice to know he's welcome, too.

Also offered are seventeen chalet-style cottages, the ones with the hot tubs. Very nice, but not for us. We ran into a couple at the golf course who were looking around for a pretty spot to have their wedding pictures taken. That's who belongs in a chalet.

The restaurant is like the rest of the lodge, with huge wooden beams and high ceilings. There is so much wood in this place, it still smells like wood, and remember, it was built in 1972. In The Timbers, even the chandeliers are wood, the work of highly skilled carpenters, with a nod to electricians. Here, as well as in other state parks, the food is uniformly good and so is the service. There is competition for our travelling dollars, and a good menu and good service are our benefits.

Enjoyed a couple huge murals on the restaurant walls, one a paddle wheeler scene and the other of a Confederate Army officer who, years ago, passed through. He didn't make it through the war, the notes read.

And just across from the restaurant is a saloon, just as brawny as the rest of the place, but free of children.

One long look at the course from the clubhouse and we realize this course plays along hills, which means to us, sidehill and downhill lies. Darn it. But that first, long, look raises unrealistic hopes, and that's why we're there; to take on this beautiful course (another Jack Kidwell design, along with a much younger Michael Hurdzan) and emerge, after eighteen holes, battered and humbled, yet still walking upright. It's the kind of view that tempts us to pass by the driving range and ignore the practice green to get to that first tee. (At your peril.)

With three par 3s on the front side, par is 71. The scorecard here is a good guide, but little more. The course plays a little over 6,000 yards, but it's one of most challenging short courses we've played. The designers weren't able to move the earth, so they found a course waiting for them, if only they could see it. They did and it includes some great and challenging doglegs. The card says that from the whites, the opening hole is a mere 372 yards. And we said, after leaving the green, "Who brought the Dramamine?" From the tee, the hole drops like a hammer and then rises like the first big hill on a roller coaster. The fairway is wide enough for two carts to drive abreast, but not much more. (A reminder not to pass up the warm-up facilities.) This green cants toward the fairway and a couple sand hazards are there.

No. 2 is only 363 yards from the whites, which starts by dropping and then rising, trees on either side guiding the approach. Suddenly, it occurs to us that club selection on this course should be unlike club selection on many other courses. The fact that your 7-iron, for example, can get you on from 150 yards on a flat course means nothing here. Switching to a 5-iron made all the difference. And as soon as we figured that out, we had a great round. (And if a 5-iron is the usual club for a 150-yard shot, reach for the utility club.)

We noted earlier that the course is open all year, weather permitting. Given the changes in elevation the cynic among us wondered aloud if, during the cold times, the fairways might be playable, but the greens snow-capped, and if that were the situation, what would green fees be?

Next we found up-and-down doglegs with stands of trees in the elbow. Drivers are important on virtually every course, but here, *placing* the tee shot often precludes its use.

Kidwell had some tricks up his sleeve when he put this course together. No. 3 is the first par 5, 464 yards and the landing area looks generous. Hah! Maybe by comparing it to the previous holes, but placement here is just as important. After the tee ball finally rolls to a stop, the journey is all uphill, accented with a dogleg. Shades of Sisyphus. With trees on both sides, at least we won't become lost.

Couple little notes we took: thank heavens for golf carts. And from almost every green (and lots of tees), the physical beauty of the course and surroundings, which includes in the distance Salt Fork Lake, makes you just stand and be grateful.

Finishing holes are among the best on the course. No. 17 is a carry over a ravine, a par 3 of 190 yards. Talk about holes where matches are won or lost, No. 17 is it. The green is long and oval, built to hold long irons or fairway woods.

And the home hole looks to the clubhouse, only 290 yards away, but as we said, so near, and yet so far. Our favorite holes were Nos. 2 and 9. We parred them.

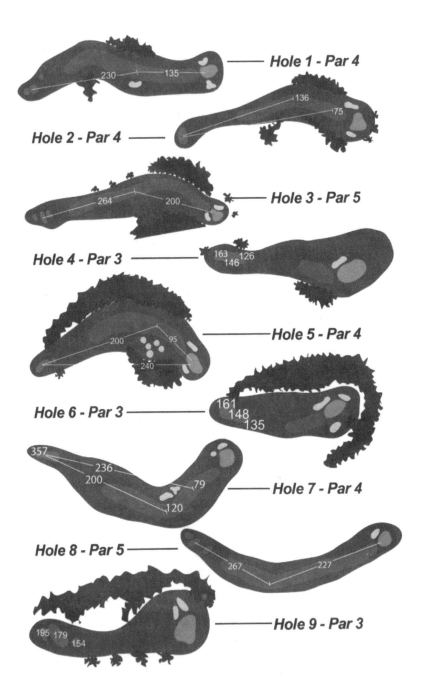

Hole 1 - Par 4

230 — 135

Hole 2 - Par 4

136

75

Hole 3 - Par 5

264 — 200

Hole 4 - Par 3

163   126
146

Hole 5 - Par 4

200   95

240

Hole 6 - Par 3

161
148
135

Hole 7 - Par 4

357
236
200
79
120

Hole 8 - Par 5

267   227

Hole 9 - Par 3

195 179
154

Salt Fork State Park

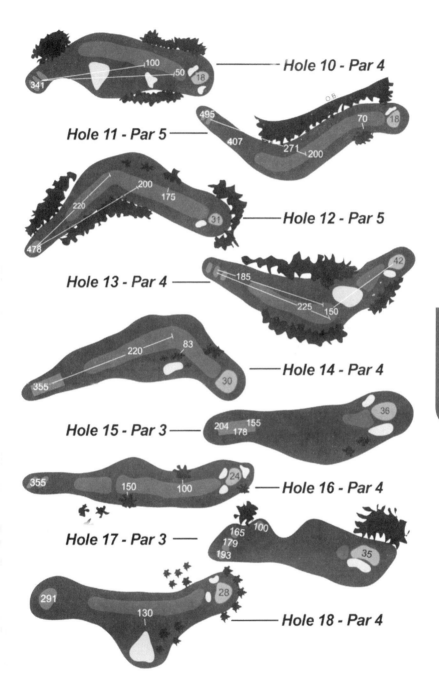

Hole 10 - Par 4

Hole 11 - Par 5

Hole 12 - Par 5

Hole 13 - Par 4

Hole 14 - Par 4

Hole 15 - Par 3

Hole 16 - Par 4

Hole 17 - Par 3

Hole 18 - Par 4

SOUTHEAST

185

Here's another neighborhood business closed down by big boxes: the owner-occupied golf repair shop.

Bend a shaft? Need grips? Want the loft on your irons beefed up? The lie adjusted for your swing? Old clubs cut down so they fit your kid? A set of custom irons?

Golf talk? No place like it. The guy(s) who run the place call you by your first name. Players with handicaps high and low stroll in and out; the shop is a wealth of local golf knowledge, and for the first-timer, it seems he stumbled into a trove of golf wisdom and experience.

Usually a pot of coffee is hot and Styrofoam cups available; sometimes the last few donuts remain from a dozen purchased earlier. Help yourself.

If there was a problem with golf repair shops, it was the difficulty of leaving them. Not unlike your neighborhood saloon, where if you didn't know everyone, at least you knew everyone's face. The usual stereotypes made for great listening: the know-it-all, the guy with everything in his bag except a swing, the rules junkie, the perfectionist, the guy who brought back stories from golf vacations in Scotland. Some of them understood the relationship between physics and hitting a golf ball.

Most left physics behind in high school and never looked back.

The incredible gobbledygook created by the marketing departments of club manufacturers is often tossed around as if we knew what we were talking about. Some of my personal favorites are, Moment of Inertia, Investment Casting, and Co-efficient of Resolution.

If I didn't know better, I would guess Moment of Inertia happens the first time a girl says "yes" to us. Investment Casting sounds like a ploy designed by bankers to draw in suckers. And if the Co-efficient of Resolution wasn't one of the lines in the recent health care debate, it should have been.

But I digress.

Two years ago, my golf shop was forced to shut its doors. Its reputation among local club professionals was sterling. It was the repair shop of choice for members of private clubs in the area. The two-time captain of the Walker Cup, Bob Lewis, and winners of the Ohio Open championship often stopped by. The executive director of the Northern Ohio PGA, Dominic Antenucci, was a regular.

MacSmith Golf was the name of the shop; it was a modest, white, cinderblock building on the east side of Cleveland.

Small indoor driving net. It was a shop, not a store. Nothing fancy.

More than a dozen years ago, I called. My problem was a Ping 3-wood, with the laminated maple head. Loved the clubhead but with a clubhead speed just a bit faster than the limit on I-71, the stiff shaft was problematic. Friends who dabbled in club repair tried to reshaft it; none was successful. Separating clubhead from shaft was impossible. In the Yellow Pages was MacSmith. I called. Bob Bando answered the phone. I said, "Can you reshaft a Ping 3-wood?" He said, "You must be from the West Side (of Cleveland)." When I replied in the affirmative, he asked, "Would you like me to do it with my eyes open or my eyes closed?"

The 3-wood was properly and perfectly reshafted and over the years, MacSmith was a regular stop for me. The driver I use today was custom-made, my sack of Haig Ultra irons was refinished, shafts were lengthened, and two gorgeous persimmon woods, a 2 and 4, from Kenneth Smith were refinished. Want to see a couple clubs so beautiful you're worried about hitting them? Take a look at these. They didn't look this good when Kenneth first finished them.

And those many, many, many hours of shop talk. Bob Bando ran the place with his father, Vic. A pair of unassuming perfectionists who, between the two of them, knew everything about golf clubs. They were well-versed in all sports and a bit partisan about Italy's contributions to art, music, tailoring, and most especially, food. Both of these Italians had married Italian women, so if they said their red sauce was the best, little was to be gained by arguing.

An added pleasure was hanging around with a father-son partnership in which each respected and enjoyed the other.

So when they broke the news, it was a sad day, indeed. Market forces don't slow for quality or craftsmanship. Market forces have a specific diet: They feed only on money.

BLACK DIAMOND GOLF COURSE AND LODGE

7500 Township Rd. 103
Millersburg
330.674.6110
www.blackdiamondgolfcourse.com

MRS. YODER'S KITCHEN

8101 State Route 241
Mount Hope
330.674.0922

The variety of courses in Ohio is impressive for golfers; for newcomers to the game it's unbelievable. Lots of players just starting to fall in love with the greatest game in the history of games ask themselves, "Where has golf been all my life?" So many courses, so little time, huh?

What type of course would you like, sir? Over here we have courses that are flat and open, just the thing as you begin the lifelong pleasure of grooving your swing. And over there, we have hilly courses, influenced by the Appalachian Mountains, and it's here you'll learn the difference between an uphill lie and downhill lie. Behind you are courses where some of the best players played: Nicklaus and Palmer, Weiskopf and Cook, Norman and Crenshaw. That's right. You're about to play the same courses, breathe the same air, and sink putts on the same greens. Want to know what it's like to play a championship course, a course equal to the private courses? Plenty of them.

Woods, hills, and water on courses are coordinated for the aesthetic beauty of the game, and the natural grace and charm provided by The Great Goddess of Golf leads atheists to become Wiccans. (When we describe courses to friends who have not yet played them, the natural attributes of the course are important parts of the story. You won't find that with tennis fanatics, now will you? They come home and say, "Gosh, you just have to see the lines on this court. I mean, they must have been painted last week." Or, "Holy Moly, love the new net.")

Ohio courses come home-made as well as made by the game's greatest designers. They can be shockingly inexpensive or put a serious dent in your Christmas Club account. After playing some courses, some new players wonder why they didn't get into sand sales. Or the selling of ball retrievers.

We're leading up to **Black Diamond Golf Course and Lodge**, because we have a few caveats before recommending the course. Designer Barry Serafin discovered and shaped this course in 2000. It is in Holmes County, the heart of Amish country, and among his design features is wheat. We don't mean the color, but the grain. Not only do fields of wheat add yet another way to define a hole, but they attract birds, too, so the wheat is an unusual and welcome two-for-one deal.

Nicklaus and Palmer, Weiskopf and Cook, Norman and Crenshaw. That's right. You're about to play the same courses, breathe the same air, and sink putts on the same greens.

Here's our one-word review of Black Diamond: spectacular. Having said that, here are the caveats:

1. It is not a course for beginners. Not to put too strong a point on it, but this track is for men who signed an Oath of Fealty to Old Tom Morris. In blood.
2. Regardless of your accuracy off the tee and with your irons, a sack of your best shag balls should be part of packing for the trip.
3. If you suffer a fear of roller coasters, stay home.
4. For at least the first few rounds here, consider suspending handicap reporting requirements.

With all the suggestions, however, we found the course spectacular. Go forth and enjoy a riotous round.

This isn't a caveat, but some advice that will help. Three sets of tees here: blue, green, and yellow. Play the yellow tees. It considerably shortens the course, but it will still be a very challenging round. When one of us was called "Yellow," he responded: "He who fights and runs away, lives to fight another day." Well put.

A round of golf on a spectacular course begins with clearing water on the first tee, starting point for the first par 5. The challenge doesn't stop there. In the middle of this uphill hole rests a boulder, about the size used to seal Jesus' grave, so you know without divine intervention, it isn't going anywhere. Mounding, up there at the green, defines the next shot and club selection. Walking off the green, thanking the guy who suggested not reporting our scores for handicaps, we found our carts out of breath and slumping a bit. No easy opening hole is this.

The fairways here are canted so much that passing a field sobriety test would be chancy. It's more than where your ball hits; it's where it stops rolling, too.

We often describe courses as being "a shotmaker's course." Here, we can take it further: It is a rifleman's course. There are no "boring" holes here, and at no point did we think we heard birdies chirping. On the other hand, we loved every minute of it. Big, big hitters welcome here. Serafin put together stone, woods, water, hills and dales, and wheat fields for this one, and we neither asked nor wanted to know what the course record is.

No. 7, a long, long par 5, appears to be impossible. It's 570 yards from the yellow tees, and a strapping 650 yards from the waybacks. Appears impossible until we realized, it is the only par 6 we've ever played. A par 6? It's the eighteenth handicap hole, but over-swinging is the norm.

No rest for the weary or wicked here. The first par 3 on the back is No. 11 and is a mere 155 yards from the middle tees, and an even shorter 120 from the yellows. Don't think it is any less demanding. Sand behind the green and plenty of water in front. This meant, for one of us, that an over-clubbed shot stopped in the sand. He was able to get out in reasonable fashion, but the ball hit the green and rolled into the water. This is our only complaint with the design. Having first given up par by landing in the sand, having a sand shot roll into water is a bit much. And we are not complainers, we add.

This course is like the best roller coaster you ever screamed upon. After getting off, you wait a minute and then say, let's go again.

We didn't say that, though, because our dinner place closes at 8 p.m.; remember, it's the middle of Amish country, not the place to look for pole dancers. The early closing has its own value. After supper, it was still light out, so we didn't have any problem navigating the country roads to get home. Closed Sundays.

The theme at **Mrs. Yoder's Kitchen** is Amish. She is going to provide generous plates of simple, delicious food, and then present a bill that makes the meal the best deal since your pediatrician gave you an ice cream cone for not crying.

It's a buffet and salad bar. Meatloaf? Real mashed? Stuff was better than Aunt Louise's, and that's saying something. Fried chicken, ham, beef a number of ways and lots of fresh veggies. We regret we were not there on a Friday, when Mrs. Yoder makes her famous baby back ribs.

Back to the course, not for midnight golf, but to grab seats on the porch of the cabin. Cabin? Geez, two of us grew up in homes smaller than this frame house.

Two-story, wrap-around porch, and three bedrooms. The fire pit is already stocked and the rowboat is all yours, if you promise to catch and release. The kitchen has everything an amateur chef needs, and there's a grill outside. Quiet you want? You won't believe how sweet the sound when the sun goes down.

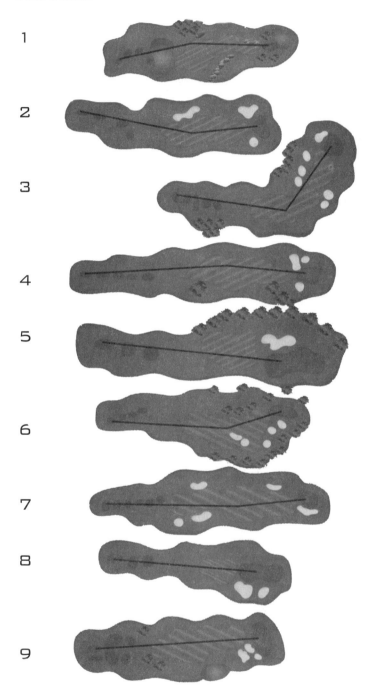

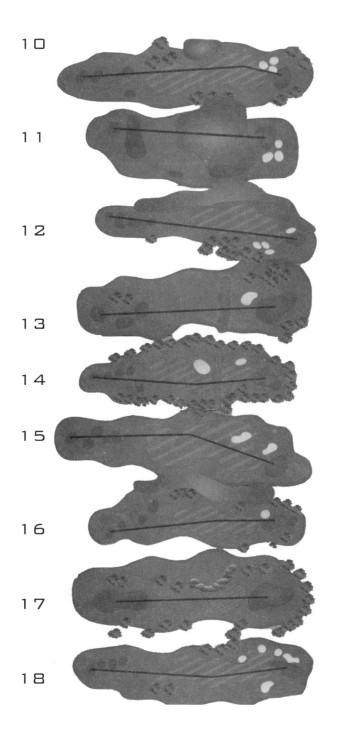

10

11

12

13

14

15

16

17

18

HORSESHOE BEND GOLF COURSE

48485 East Captina Hwy.
Armstrong Mills
740. 686.2351
www.horseshoebendgolfcourse.com

HAMPTON INN

51130 National Rd.
Saint Clairsville
740.695.3961

How could you not like a course called **Horseshoe Bend Golf Course** in a town called Armstrong Mills? Sounds as if there are rifle scabbards on the sides of golf bags. It is surrounded by Captina Creek and more than that, in every direction tree-covered hills rise. You can go here in the fall, but be warned: a couple days in this natural paradise and you're going to start pricing double-wides and tell your wife to send a copy of *Walden* to see if you and Thoreau are fellow travelers.

The fun here is found on the course, which is eminently playable. A noticeable lack of sand and only two water hazards, very good maintenance, small greens, and the woods that hem it all in. The owners are a husband and wife team, Randy and Nancy Boan.

It was a friend who inspired Randy to build a golf course. Fred Dillon would stop every so often, crack a cold one and admire the property, which was in the Boan family and used for farming. When Fred looked at the property, he told Randy, he saw a golf course. Few years later, Randy started researching golf course design and maintenance. Next thing you know, naming rights are on the to-do list. Well, if you look at the course on a map, you see the creek that goes around the property and it resembles a horseshoe. (Tip: If you meet Alan Boan, the 21-year-old son of the owner, don't play him for anything more than dimes. His handicap index is 1.7, and he shot the course record, 60. That score was witnessed by his mom, who last season fired her first ace, on No. 13.)

Greens are bent and the rest is blue. Generous landing areas, but getting on in regulation calls for the skills of a dart thrower with the irons. Snack shop with the basics.

Last season, Randy was about to mow a green when he saw hoof prints in it. Repairing ball marks left by rude golfers is one thing. This was something else. He's a hunter and fisherman, but had never seen the print before. His educated guess was buffalo. He was right. The shaggy old guy was part of a herd owned by a local man. Son Alan recalls a player commenting, "Heard you got buffalo on the course," probably a line never heard at any golf club this side of Mississippi. The buffalo was never seen by Randy or Alan, but left plenty of circumstantial and forensic evidence. The old guy turned up on the other side of the railroad tracks. Too bad he wasn't able to stay a few days. Think of the questions to be resolved with the rule book.

Lots of wildlife enjoys life here, and if you keep an eye peeled, you might come across the nest of a red-shouldered hawk. They apparently like the variety of trees as much as we do; the nest might be in a sycamore, tulip tree, white oak or river birch.

Staying at the **Hampton Inn**, in St. Clairsville, is the best idea, despite it being twenty miles from the course. First of all, those are twenty beautiful miles, two-lane blacktop of country road. It's a pleasure to do the speed limit and traffic jams here are heard of, but never seen.

Even better, the Hampton seems designed for golfers on getaways. The usual stuff is there, of course, pool and workout room, computer access, free hot breakfast, comfortable rooms to sit and say, "Shut up and deal." There are 116 rooms here, but only one suite.

Those hills? The Hampton sits on one of the highest, so the views enjoyed on the course and on the drive now get another look from a different perspective.

It gets better.

In addition to location and amenities, the Hampton has a good Italian restaurant and an equally good sports bar. You punch third floor on the elevator and when the doors open, to the left is Undo's and to the right is the Sports Bar. One of our group thought he had died and gone to heaven. Another noted we didn't need a designated driver.

At the Sports Bar, the theme is men, the gender which eats with its fingers, so the brief menu includes chicken wings, flat bread pizza and the like, paired with cold beer. If there is a game to be had, it's on the telly here.

The two facilities are separately owned. Pictures of the Undo family are on the wall leading to the restaurant, which has a great touch with salads (huge, cold, and colorful) and bread (warm, crusty, just waiting for butter), and a very good red sauce. There are always specials, so if you see someone enjoying chicken cacciatore but don't see it on the menu, that's probably among the specials. It's one of those places where, sooner or later, every guy in the joint loosens his belt.

When The Guy is putting together this outing, he knows better than to pair born-agains with agnostics, union with management, PETA with hunters, snorers and non-snorers, and perhaps most importantly, who loves garlic and who doesn't. Garlic lovers should bunk only with other garlic lovers. The chef at Undo's has a heavy hand with garlic, may God bless and keep him.

What a place—drinks, dinner and clean sheets, all under the same roof. And on the course—incredible scenery, opportunities for pars and birdies, the odd buffalo, and a red-shouldered hawk watching over you.

Horseshoe Bend Golf Course

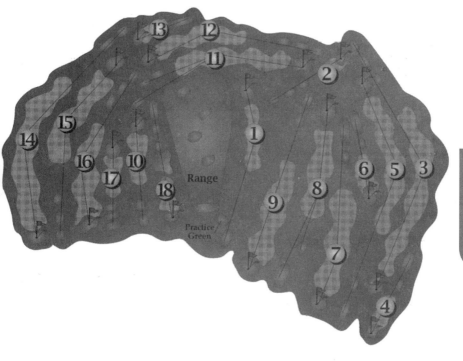

SOUTHEAST

197

Oxbow Golf Club

500 St. Andrews Blvd.

Belpre

800.423.0443

www.oxbow-golf.com

Lafayette Hotel Marietta

101 Front St.

Marietta

740.373.5522

www.lafayettehotel.com

Holiday Inn

701 Pike St.

Marietta

740.374.9660

Stockport Mill Inn

1995 Broadway St.

Stockport

740.559.2822

www.stockportmill.com

Marietta Country Club

705 Pike Street

Marietta

740.373-7722

www.mariettacc.org

The lodging, dining, and golf prospects for a getaway to Marietta are varied, but we made our first stop to a graveyard. (We noticed, making our way to the boneyard, that this town must have been laid out by engineers; every street meets the next at a ninety-degree angle.)

Not just any graveyard. It is Mound Cemetery, on Fifth and Scammel streets. It was created long before Mounds candy bars were prized in every Halloween bag. Way before. We don't even know how old the mound is, though best guess is between 100 B.C. and 400 A.D. This mound is thirty feet high, conical in shape, and has steps pushed into the side so we can walk to the top. Two things: one, you're standing on prehistory and the bones of some long-dead chieftains, and two, thoughts of immortality are not suffered here.

A little inside skinny: Naughty Marietta is the name of an operetta. (Funny what you learn when you're on the road.) Marietta, Ohio is the Ohio River town named for the French queen Marie Antoinette. You might remember from your sixth grade history class that France was invaluable as we parted company with England.

Marietta is a handsome, little, college town. A river town too, where the Ohio River takes on the Muskingum River before its date with destiny: the Mississippi. On one side is Ohio, and West By God Virginia on the other. On an irregular basis, the river floods.

On previous trips we've enjoyed the **Lafayette Hotel Marietta**, hard by river's edge, where the restaurant is called the Gun Room. A selection of long rifles decorates the walls. If history is part of a getaway, this place is noteworthy. If there are six or more sitting for dinner, don't worry about figuring the tip; they figure it for you, with no consultation regarding service, and it's a very generous 18 per cent. The menu is pretty much split between beef and fish, and the beef includes a flat iron steak, an unusual-looking (rectangular) cut fast becoming popular for its flavor and tenderness. Interesting, because the three-sided hotel is sometimes referred to as a flat iron building.

More handsome is the Riverview Lounge, where the menu is a bit more casual and the theme is riverboat. Hello, again, Bart and Bret Maverick.

Given the age of the hotel (it's pushing 100), no surprise that the rooms are compact. Comfortable, but compact. If you, Bart, Bret, and the rest of the group want to play cards, we suggest a suite for The Guy.

Tee it up at **Oxbow Golf Club**, in nearby Belpre. Oxbow Golf & Country Club was designed by Jack Kidwell and the guy he handed the design baton to, Michael Hurdzan. That was in 1974. Kidwell is at the Big Driving Range in the Sky and Hurdzan continues to amaze players with his courses. In 1974, courses were often created with big greens, which present two concerns. First, getting on doesn't mean getting down in regulation. Especially here, where lots of them are two-tiered. Second, big greens mean big expense for the superintendent. And here, they are not just big, they're fast. Playing the first time around is experimental; we didn't keep score. Just as well. The less talented putters in the group kept saying, "If it wasn't for the speed and direction, that would have been a good putt." We've heard that before. The course record is a very impressive 64 and one has to believe the putter was magical that round. The course was in need of a shave and a haircut, so before you schedule anything, call the course and ask a few questions about current maintenance status.

From the blues, it's 6,558 yards; from the whites, a more manageable 6,216 yards. Par is 71. No. 13 at Oxbow is a short par 3 that is heavily wooded, including the back of the green. The woods are thick enough to think about *Where the Wild Things Are*. If we had to make a mistake in club selection, it would be on the short side. Sand on the right isn't as much of a hazard here as it is a help in stopping the ball from any further damage. However, hitting a sand shot isn't easy. Overhit it and it's going to roll off the green into the deep, dark woods. A hole where you extol the many virtues of the scramble format.

Sand and water enough to keep attention on the game, and No. 18, 402 yards from the whites, trudges inexorably toward the clubhouse and the critical eyes behind the glass.

Another place to rest our weary bones, slake our thirst, and plow through a stack of beefsteaks is up the road a piece, the **Stockport Mill Inn**, which first came to life as a feed mill and still has its original grain elevator. The grain bin, thoroughly swept up, is now the massage therapy room.

Suites and rooms here, each striking and very, very comfortable. This one you're not going to believe: an elegant suite for eight, fewer if modesty is an issue. The heck with modesty, the Captain Hook suite has large screen telly, six-man hot tub (again, the modesty issue), small kitchen with poker table dining table and chairs, and terrace overlooking the dam. One more thing: a private staircase to the cupola, named the Eagle Watch. For good reason: American eagles live in the area, notable for their noble faces, huge wing spans and rickety nests. If one glides by, you'll stand and salute. Dinner only, Fridays and Saturdays only, and on Sunday, belly buster brunch. The breads are homemade and the produce comes from nearby farms. Finally, some good tomatoes in a restaurant.

In addition, the **Holiday Inn** here has, among others, a package with the **Marietta Country Club**, and we've always liked Holiday Inns and private clubs, so if rubbing shoulders with the landed gentry is appealing, this getaway is worth exploring.

If there is a more handsome clubhouse than this, we haven't seen it. It isn't new. It was originally built and used as a barn for the dairy farm here. When the club was created, the barn served as the equipment shed. A few decades ago, fire destroyed the original clubhouse and visionary members looked to the barn. A huge renovation, of course, and some additions, but they saved and found a new use for a historic and beautiful structure.

The course here is private club quality, and improvements are constantly considered and made. If you wonder how the course looks so healthy, one of the recent projects was a computer-driven irrigation system.

It is not a long course, topping out at a tad more than 6,000 yards, par 70. That doesn't mean easy. But it does offer generous landing areas along with championship-caliber greens. Too bad it's a thinking man's course; it's easy to become distracted with the natural beauty. Dawdling is understandable, but not permissible.

Not only does the hotel have a getaway with the private club, but dining privileges are included, too. After a couple rounds and couple dinners here, you might add club membership to your Christmas list.

Here's Hilton lagniappe—if you stay here, you get privileges at the YMCA, too. We recommend, for purposes of poker and fellowship, the spacious executive room for The Guy.

The hotel sixty-seat restaurant is Memories (and, please, don't sing it, hum it, or think about it) and its twelve-ounce strip is noteworthy. Even more flavorful is the baby back ribs, a dish that has garnered a number of prizes. If your cholesterol is as low as your score, they offer onion petals, too. Here's a little tip that provides comfort: Ask your waiter to wet your napkin with hot water. Trust me, you'll use it and wonder why you didn't figure this out yourself.

The bar is Brandy's, and again, no singing. It wasn't named for "…what a good wife you would be," but for the last couple of bosses there. At least that's the story we got. One guy was Brad and the other was Andy. This square bar was clearly the inspiration for Cheers. Any minute you think Norm is going to shuffle through the door and down the steps. All together now, "NORM!"

A mere sixty years ago, the Ohio legislature created the Department of Natural Resources. Talk about your foresight. In addition to an incredible amount of property and to the myriad programs it administers (and they are very, very impressive) are a half dozen state lodges with golf courses.

Not just any golf courses, either. *Golf Digest* lists them in its "Places to Play." As if we needed to be pushed in that direction. The courses have garnered enough stars from the magazine that, put together, we could read outdoors at night.

The late designer Jack Kidwell designed the first five golf courses and Arthur Hills designed the most recent. About 115,000 rounds are played every season. Without exception, course maintenance and conditioning is superb.

Details are scattered throughout the book, but our general impression of the staff and lodges might be noteworthy. Staff at each place was professional and praiseworthy. The lodges themselves, from Tudor to modern, were beautiful. Offering cottages to nomads such as us? Brilliant.

Here's another thing that might go unnoticed: peace. Staying at a state park means being as close to nature as we're going to get for a while. We forget how beautiful it is. Staying in a lodge or cottage is so peaceful, so refreshing, and so relaxing, as to be therapeutic. No rush hour, no parking meters, no pick-up-the-dry-cleaning-get-the-oil-changed-lecture-the-kids-about-drugs-and-alcohol-and-don't-forget-your-anniversary-is-tomorrow.

Just some camaraderie, cold beers, good food, and lots and lots of great golf.

WINDY KNOLL
GOLF CLUB
500 Roscommon Dr.
Springfield
937.390.8898
www.windyknollgolfclub.com

MARRIOTT COURTYARD
& MÉLA URBAN BISTRO
100 South Fountain Ave.
Springfield
937.322.3600

Say you're a wind player? Welcome to **Windy Knoll Golf Club,** where the flags are only five feet tall. Any taller and a gust can pull them out of the cups. On this gorgeous and playable track, the wind is a factor. Not a big one, but it's there and the best scores are turned in by the guys who have figured it out.

This isn't the place to say, "Whaddya mean? Of course my 5-iron goes 170—watch." This is the place to wet a finger, stick it in the air and say, "Let's see, that's a club-and-a-half-wind. If I come up short, I'll be okay, but if I fly the green, I'm in the trap and the green slopes forward."

And some commoners think golf is not a thinking man's game. Fools!

Windy Knoll's logo is a stylized horse head and that has good reason, too—the course is laid out over what once was a horse farm. Not just any horse farm, but a breeding farm for thoroughbreds.

Reminders are constant; horseshoes used as tee markers and holes with names from horse racing. No. 1 is the Starting Gate, No. 6 is Along the Rail, No. 17 is Home Stretch. The maintenance buildings were first used as barns. The most striking design element is grazing horses. Not real ones, of course, but realistic horse statues created by a Columbus artist. Players enjoying the course for the first time do double-takes, followed by squinting their eyes and waiting for some movement. They aren't the only ones. Residents have called the police to report escaped horses. It's a rare player who packs a camera in his bag, but in this case, it's a good idea.

Designer Brian Huntley was given 350 acres to work with, a generous tract of land. He dished out seventy-six strategic bunkers and left five holes with none. No shortage of water, which adds to thinking about wind, club selection and the risk and reward. It is a thinking man's course, and that's just the way it was designed.

Four sets of tees: black, grey, white, and burgundy. One unnoticed change in golf design is the abandonment of three tees and colors: red, white and blue. Now tees are set for older players, front tees, member tees and the waybacks. Good designers spend as much time at the waybacks as the forward tees. Your hands should be manicured as well as this course.

Nothing tricked up about the greens. Getting on the dance floor is the challenge. If you play well tee to green, it's a satisfying round, but don't forget the hazards, including wind. Oh, and don't forget the fescue. An errant drive or shot can land in this stuff, obviously created by the Goddess of Golf to drive players nuts. In prime growing season, this ball-consuming grass is taller than two-year old boys and equally temperamental. The intermediate rough is playable though making par becomes a risky bet. Windy Knoll is built on flat terrain and that means level lies. And who doesn't love a level lie?

And some commoners think golf is not a thinking man's game. Fools!

We think the fescue was planted for an additional purpose: beauty. It provides depth and definition to the course on this rolling terrain. The course bills itself as a links-style course and has three elements of links courses: short flags, wind, and fescue. Other than that, it's no more a links course than your Aunt Louise was a race car driver. She had three elements, too: a car, a lead foot and a deep desire to go faster than anyone else.

Windy Knoll can be played as long as 6,800 yards, but the waybacks are not recommended for the first couple trips around this track; after that, the low handicap players will have a good idea of the influence of the wind and be able to confidently take on this sneaky-tough course. The superintendent and crew, by the way, get an A+ for maintaining and manicuring this track. Not an easy task when mounding and heather are in play.

Opened in 2002, greens are settled and able to hold shots. The greens are all sand, a nod to Carolina golf, and they are all faster than they appear. As in every match, the guy with the best short game will win.

Only two greens, Nos. 3 and 10, give pause with their easy-to-see breaks, and after playing them a few times, they are greens to look forward to. The rest roll gently, which is not to say they are easy.

No. 2 reminds us of the value of warming up. A long par 3 (178 yards from the whites, 188 yards from the greys), but the target is a very big green, and the second par 3 on this side is equally long and shows up early: No. 4, 174 yards from the whites, 211 from the greys, and this is the first time players have to stick finger in mouth, hold hand in air, and decide: what's that wind going to do to the ball?

Back up a bit because the No. 3 hole is a relatively short par 5 at only 476 yards from the whites, 492 yards from the greys. Well, ol' Brother Huntley is not going to present us with a straightaway par 5, now is he? So going for it in two is often tempting, but missing the green will haul you back to reality with all the gentleness of a cyclone (fast, furious, and leaving you saying, "what the heck was that?"). Nos. 2,4, and 5 can define the front side of the round, so if the decision on these tees is between raising the bet or checking, check.

We loved No. 8, a short par 4, only 271 yards from the whites and 287 yards from the greys, so the green is a siren to both the brave and the foolish. Designer Huntley shows the way and at the same time shows us where we'll be if we don't hit the perfect drive: the Badlands of Springfield. Sand offered in two varieties: steep-sided bunkers and flat. If we stay the sirens, and get on in regulation, the rolling green means it still isn't a kick-in.

Having survived the trial by fire of the front nine, the back side gets even better. No. 10 is lined with trees, a short 330 yards from the greys and an even shorter 315 yards from the whites, finished with a pretty exciting green, our way of saying your approach better be good.

Speaking of mounding, it's a design tool that works well on flat courses and adds a lot to this course. Whether used for bunkering or to provide a membership bounce, it seems to us a more important function is to provide players with depth perception and along the way, mounding adds both beauty and drama.

Home hole is one of the best, a par 5 that reminds us it ain't over 'til it's over. We like finishing with par 5s because in a close match, the opportunity (risk) for a two-shot swing (reward) is often present. Water, sand, trees and 530 yards from the greys and 511 yards from the whites. The green is a big one; this is no time to stop concentrating.

We think the course is cause for celebration for this reason: It doesn't have to stretch more than 7,000 yards to be a great golf challenge. Also, so many of the holes are memorable. We played from the grey tees and the whites, the player on the white tees being a high handicapper. He picked the right tee and loved the course. There's a lesson there.

For the first round at Windy Knoll, the course is the teacher. For subsequent rounds, the player is studious yet confident. We know that because instead of heading home the next day, we played the track again. It was worth arriving home after dinner.

Marriott Courtyard is likely one of the nicest places in Springfield, a very pretty town. Rooms are bright, comfortable, and functional. To ante up, the king suite is the place. The important things are provided, such as wake-up calls and semi-firm beds. For those who still enjoy the many delights of nicotine, there is the courtyard. And this Marriott has one more benefit, its restaurant, **Méla Urban Bistro**. Or, as they like to say, Méla's Urban Bistro.

Going after a round? Shower and put on your better slacks and shirt. Blazer if you have one. Only seventy-eight places at the tables here, and the floor-to-ceiling arch windows are a handsome addition.

We ordered the chicken arrabiata for one reason and one reason only: We love to roll our tongues and say arrabiata. We don't have any idea what it means, but we know this: said properly, you feel like a swashbuckler. The plate had at least a half dozen representatives from the list of major food groups and pointed out how a good chef can take something as boring as a chicken breast and make it flavorful. We also ordered excellent lamb chops and we ordered those for one reason and one reason only: It's a plate not served at home. Wish we could have enjoyed a couple appetizers (here, they are called preludes), but we're not the trenchermen we used to be.

They don't serve drinks here; you order cocktails. Excellent bar service, by the way. Walking out after dinner, we breathed deeply and said, "Springfield, Ohio?" Finding this place in this very pretty small town goes to the top of the list marked, Serendipity. Purely wonderful.

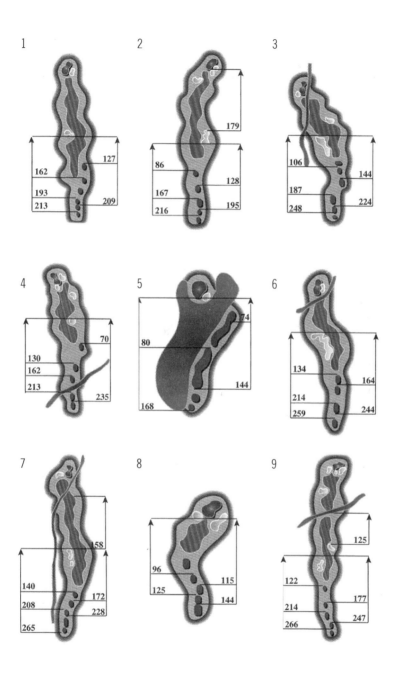

1

127
162
193
209
213

2

179
86
128
167
195
216

3

106
144
187
224
248

4

70
130
162
213
235

5

74
80
144
168

6

134
164
214
244
259

7

158
140
172
208
228
265

8

96
115
125
144

9

125
122
177
214
247
266

Windy Knoll Golf Club

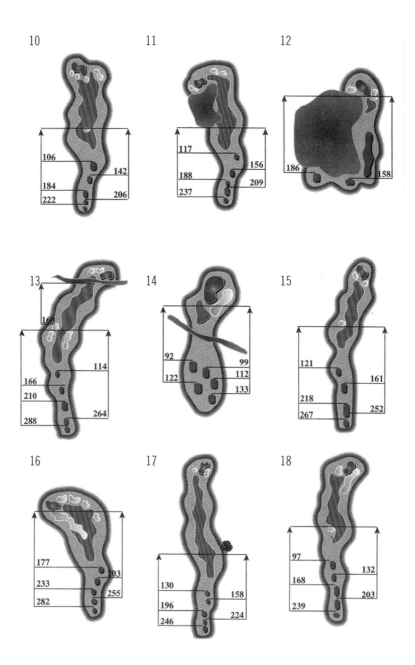

HUESTON WOODS STATE PARK

6301 Park Office Rd.
College Corner
800.282.7275
www.huestonwoodsstateparklodge.com

INDIAN RIDGE GOLF CLUB

2600 Oxford Millville Rd.
Oxford
877.426.8365
www.indianridgegolfclub.com

HUESTON WOODS GOLF COURSE

6962 Brown Rd.
Oxford
513.523.8081

Funny what will stay with you after a getaway. At **Hueston Woods Golf Course,** we were talking with a staff member about the course and he told us a great piece of gossip. The regular players in this southwest state park regularly suggest to club management that there be no publicity, no marketing, no p.r. about the course. They have it just the way they want it and the fewer outsiders who know about it, the better. Sharing the wealth is clearly not among their virtues.

With more than 3,000 acres, the park is the pride of College Corner, unless you happen to be an alum from nearby Miami (of Ohio) University, in Oxford. Even then, the park is held is in high esteem; many of its employees are students. Important as the work done by the state, maybe even more important work was what the state didn't do. The state didn't hack away with a preconceived vision of the park; instead, thought was given to accommodating Mother Nature, the better to enjoy Her. The result is a state park where hikers are delighted and fishermen are in all their glory. (The park brags about fossil hunting, too, which is taking genealogy to the nth degree.)

The lodge is like the rest of the lodges at state parks: magnificent.

Almost made us feel like pikers when we took cottages. That meant no gazing out on Lake Acton, named for Clyde Acton, who was the state legislator held responsible for damming a stream until the lake was big enough for sailboats and fishermen. This might be another example of where legislators' strengths lie. The park wraps around the shoreline. The lodge is above the lake and makes better viewing than anything on television.

Pikers we were until we found two of the cottages are suites with master bedrooms. If the last hand is dealt at 1:30 in the morning, better that beds be close by.

Long before that ancient call is sounded, "Ante up," we sat around the restaurant, Trailblazers, eating and drinking as if we were landed gentry. One of us, after dilly-dallying over the menu, reminded us what a melting pot is America. From the appetizer section were offers from China (pot stickers), Greece (spanakopeta), Italy (mozzarella and marinara sauce), and France (onion soup). To that reminder, another one of us did a bad imitation of the old bat in the Wendy's commercials, who leaned over the counter and demanded, "Where's the beef?"

Beef? It's beef you want? Trailblazers has enough beef to justify its own cattle pen. The filet mignon is bigger than most, eight ounces. We had two Delmonicos, and there are also sirloins to be had. On weekends, they roast and slice prime rib.

Minor complaint here, though it's not really about Trailblazers; it's about offering Classic Caesar on the menu. It's been a couple decades or more since we've had a real Caesar. Two main ingredients are raw egg and anchovies, and now that industrial farming has made our eggs suspect, no one is going to use them in the raw form. Et tu?

The course played by the regulars, those selfish galoots, is a wonderful getaway course: far from the madding crowds and surrounded by mature woodlands, the only sound louder than persimmon meeting balata is a woodpecker preparing lunch. It is one of those rare courses that has a mascot. In this case, a real one, a wild turkey known as Wishbone. Ol' Wishbone hasn't been seen recently, and there is turkey hunting in the park.

Driving range and putting green are there for those who need to warm up, and get this—in addition to riding carts, pull carts are available. The course is more than walkable; it's a joy to walk here. (This always leads us to ask the unanswerable: Why isn't play faster with riding carts?)

Jack Kidwell designed this course, which opened in 1969. He had 260 acres to work with; the raw materials were there in abundance. Plus, he didn't have a developer leaning over his shoulder, telling him, "Jack, you have that dogleg par 5 crossing what will be a cul-de-sac with McMansions. Move it."

Kidwell presents us with a course that can favor the big boomers, 7,044 yards from the tips, or challenge the new guy, 5,251 yards from the forwards. The whites are long, too, at 6,718 yards, which proved to be more golf course than we were players. The par 3s, even from the whites, are championship lengths. No. 3 is 182 yards; No. 8 is 172 yards. On the back side, No. 16 is 195 yards, most of it carry over water, and the home is the last par 3, this one 192 yards. Or as we said, "Geez, Mr. Kidwell, just because you had a lot of property doesn't mean you had to use it all. A hundred and fifty yards would have been just fine."

The course is no stranger to competitive play; winners of the Ohio Open, State Women's Amateur, and the MAC championship took home trophies from here.

Don't take this to mean the driver will be used on every tee. There are thirty sand bunkers, which is plenty, as far as we're concerned, and water comes into play from four ponds. We got the feeling that Kidwell wanted to build a very good course, but didn't want it to interfere with the woods, the big stands of maples and beech that anchor the course and play a role more important than grass type. (Which is, incidentally, bent on tees and greens, and a combination blue and rye elsewhere.)

Some courses are created, some are discovered. Hueston Woods was discovered among the farmland and woods, and designed in deference to Mother Nature.

Just up the road a piece is **Indian Ridge Golf Club**, a Brian Huntley design that should be included on any trip to the area.

Whatever sand wasn't used by Jack Kidwell on the Hueston Woods course must have been stored until Huntley decided where he wanted bunkers. There are fifty-nine in all, and when combined with four elegant lakes, the wages of sinful swings are bogeys. We called the design sleek, because it has the wonderful country club look to it; bent grass, greens measuring 10.5 on the Stimp and only 6,022 yards from the member tees. Plus, Indian Ridge is spread over 180 acres, so there's no crowding. That's not to say it can't play lots longer than that; from the tips, it's 7,001 yards and the course record is a sparkling 64.

Here's a little inside skinny: The back side plays three shots harder than the front. Be aware. Here's more: if the wind is behind you on No. 7, go for it. It's a short par 4, only 291 yards, but much of that is carry, plus the fairway bunker is really in the fairway. It stretches the width of the green and between bunker and green is some fairway. If the wind is in your face, Mother Nature is telling you, "Oh, don't be foolish." If your playing partners are questioning your manhood and insisting you go for it, well, now you know who your friends are.

Trees come into play, but more on the last six holes. They can be a factor in the increased difficulty of the back side, but so is No. 14. Geez—listen to what's between your drive and rattling the cup: It's a par 5, 487 yards, downhill, dogleg left, and there's water in front of the green. It will take you as long to describe the hole as it took to play it.

THE GOLF CLUB AT STONELICK HILLS

3155 Sherilyn Ln.
Batavia
513.735.4653
www.stonelickhills.com

ELK'S RUN GOLF CLUB

2000 Elklick Rd.
Batavia
513.735-6600
www.elksrun.com

FLEMING'S PRIME STEAKHOUSE

4432 Walnut St.
Batavia
937.320.9548

HOLIDAY INN EXPRESS

301 Old Bank Rd.
Milford
513.831.7829

The Golf Club at Stonelick Hills, in Batavia, plays long: From the tips, it's 7,145 yards, from the gold, 6,817 yards, even from the blue tees, it's 6,483 yards. The forward tees are 5,116 yards. All that may be according to the laser measuring system, but no one has ever praised our shotmaking as laser-like. Ah, so what? The course is the best in parkland design and between the woods and the water, if adding snorkeling gear and a Poulan chainsaw to the bag make sense, we'd play it again and again.

We were standing on the second tee, knocked out with the physical beauty of the course, when one of us proclaimed, "Livin' high off the hog, we are. High off the hog." He got no argument.

We agreed that if a course can't begin with a par 5, a good, short par 4 is second best. This one is especially good because it's a dogleg. The difference? A reachable par 4 is too tempting for many players, and the risk, this early in the game, isn't worth the reward. Ergo, drivers are left in the bag. This hole offers a wide landing area and clear directions to the green. A big, flat green it is, so starting off with a par is doable and a birdie is a distinct possibility.

No. 3 is the first par 3. Beautiful. It was a pleasant surprise getting to the tee and looking at the lake that separates tee from green. Not long, but a poor swing can light the afterburners on a score. Our collective advice: Just. Get. On. The. Green.

The first par 5, like the first par 4, is a short one. It was doubtless inspired by a water moccasin traversing the lake surface. For almost all of us, it's a three-shotter, and a demanding one at that. For those rare birds who can actually stroke an accurate, long drive, along with a great second shot, an eagle beckons. Getting in the way of a great drive, though, is a serious fairway bunker and to the left of it, Sherwood Forest. And protecting the green is a phalanx of sand ambushes, the Swiss Guards of bunkers. Still, one of the pleasures of golf is watching other players hit heroic shots, so encouraging The Guy Who Would Eagle is usually a good idea.

No. 7 is another good risk-and-reward tee. Take the land route and par 4 is not difficult. Take the water route and you're a gambler. A dogleg right and that body of water is in the elbow. If the shot is successful, though, you get a much better look at a difficult green as well as a two- or three-club advantage over the landlubbers.

The finishing hole on the front side is another water hole, and magnificent: Water to the right, water to the left, and an island green. A reasonably long par 5 and big hitters, on approaching their second shot, hear in the distance, "The whole world is watching … The whole world is watching … The whole world is watching." That strident, disconcerting chant comes from the clubhouse. The view from the porch looks down No. 9, and everyone there wants to watch you go for it. It's a little easier the second time around, because by that time, the green looks bigger. It should; at 11,000 square feet., it's almost as big as the clubhouse.

Food in the clubhouse at Stoney's Pub is the best clubhouse food ever. Period. The guy who designed and built this course had a background in food service, and it shows. We split a couple eight-ounce cheeseburgers and wolfed down four salads before venturing back to our carts. And we wondered: This is a new and killer course. Property that Mother Nature would be proud to call Her own. Staff that treats us like cousins, good rates, open all year, and yet, something was missing. Ah, slapping our foreheads. Where is the housing development?

There ain't any. We go by houses when we pull in, but there are none on the course. That's by design. The only language spoken here is golf.

Speaking of design, here are a few more elements that added to the fun. The finishing greens on both sides are close to the clubhouse. Not to make the journey quicker, but to allow porch sitters to get a better view of us as we putt. Not just any seats on that porch, either. You know how your Aunt Louise would tell you when one door is closed, another opens? In this case, the old bat was right as rain. The same year Riverfront Stadium was leveled, Stonelick Hills opened. The dedication round was played in the middle of summer, 2004. From the home of the Big Red Machine, twenty seats were rescued, and that's what we sat on to watch players finishing.

Here's the part you're not going to believe. The Stonelick Hills business doesn't seek profit. True. Profits are plowed back into the club and course. Know why? Because management has the loftiest goal in Ohio golf: Stonelick Hills seeks to become the finest public course and club in the state. Cue up the sound track from *Exodus*.

We digress. The second nine piles on more of the same. No. 10 is one of those par 5s we refer to as tremendous (guys who walk away with a par), challenging (guys who walk off with a bogey), or brutal (guys who pencil in not a number, but a letter, D, and it stands for disaster). Once again, thank goodness for the handicap system, which allows only so many strokes on the scorecard, a number determined by handicap. For most players, it means no worse than a seven.

It's a dogleg left, with some water on the right and woods on the left. Water shouldn't come into play. More than play this hole, you stalk it. We didn't find this par 5 to be a place to pick up a birdie; we found it to be a par 5 that called for five consecutive good shots. Especially the approach and two putts.

No. 11 is another great, short par 4. Fail to select the right stick at the tee and suddenly, you hear your mother's voice, "How many times do I have to tell you?" Sharp dog left. Lots and lots of water right. Sandman in the elbow.

The home hole is not only demanding, it's dramatic, too. And knowing the guys sitting on the Riverfront seats are the ones chanting, "The whole world is watching ... The whole world is watching," adds a dollop of stage fright. But played without ego, it's a wonderful finishing hole. A par 5 with water left and right, both of which come into play, and bunkers enough to give pause. Whew.

We quoted Ernie Banks when we finished. "Let's play two!"

We stayed at the **Holiday Inn Express** in Milford. Handsome place and from a distance, could pass as a church. We've always enjoyed Holiday Inns, considering them the heavy lifters of the hotel business. They are geared for families and business meetings. But with just a tad of creativity, setting up the Batavia World Series of Golf is a simple matter. Some Holiday Inns are better than others, of course, but for golf getaways, they have always worked well. And this one, in Milford, is an Express, which means that on the way out the front door, we can grab a very nutritious, equally tasty, and simple breakfast. No bacon and eggs or biscuits and sausage gravy for us. We want to be strong when we tee it up. Breakfast is included in the price, too. (Incidentally, because we had such a good, low-fat breakfast at the hotel, we splurged on the burgers at the turn. Seemed to work well.) Any of the suites here work well for a card game, but the jacuzzi suite is pure prime. Just the room for The Guy.

This Holiday Inn is rich. Friendly staff, good at checking in-and-checking-out, and blessed with two great golf courses and a steakhouse that serves prime beef.

Somebody say prime? When the beef is prime, it's time to order filet mignons. It's always a nice cut, but God didn't design the filet to be the most flavorful. But with prime, you get as good as you're going to get. At **Fleming's Prime Steakhouse**, two are offered, an eight ounce and a twelve-ounce. The menu is a la carte, which is French for "bet you clean this plate," because there are no included extras. You want an extra? It goes on your tab. Fleming's opened just a few years ago and all cylinders are smoothly firing. We had perfectly-grilled filets and the only extra we ordered was the justly-famous Fleming's potato. You won't get this at home: baked tater with sour cream, cheddar cheese, and jalapenos. One guy at the table ate his beef before moving to the spud. Why? He thought the spud's flavor might overwhelm the flavor of the steak. He spoke highly of both items. Full bar, of course.

The other course was designed by none other than Greg Norman, the egomaniac who collapsed en route to winning the Masters. Ah, how the mighty can fall. Lots of fans experienced Schadenfreude that fateful Sunday in spring. Hey, that was then and this is now and even though he likely trades on his name more than his design experience, **Elk's Run Golf Club** is green and good-looking, great fun and challenging from the right tees. We like to trade on Norman's name, too. As in, "Oh, yeah, I played the Norman course and he must think everyone can put spin on the ball like he can."

He certainly got a great piece of land to work with; mature forests and rolling hills, and the result won't surprise anyone: the track is beautiful. Very well maintained, too. He added hazards with sod walls and greens that have more play in them than most four-year olds. Front side is more open that the back. Lots of water, too, and most of it comes into play.

It opens with a par 4 of 335 yards (only 353 yards from the tips, so two relaxed swings and you're wondering, "Am I going to birdie the first hole on a Norman course?") The answer, yes, you are, my boy. But don't let it go to your head. The first par 3 follows immediately, and it's 175 yards and no running it up. Bunkered on front and both sides.

On the card, the next hole, the first par 5, isn't long at 508 yards, but if a power fade or slice is your shot of choice from the tee (or from the fairway), tee up a shag ball. Water on the right will take both shots. And, yes, one of us plunked the drive and then the second in water. On the other hand, a good drive makes the next shot tempting. As in, "Hmm. Could I get on a Norman par 5 in two?" The answer is, yes, you can, my boy.

Elk's Run Golf Course is green and good-looking, great fun and challenging from the right tees.

Risks and rewards are easy to discern here and the course isn't as overwhelming as it strategic. The second par 3, No. 8, plays only 136 yards, but the fairway is going to drop substantially and missing the green is the result of poor club selection.

We loved No. 10 because if you can't land your tee shot in the middle of the fairway, bogeys beckon, and it's a short par 4 in the first place, 355 yards. No. 12 can be the source for a puffed-up chest, or a head hanging in shame. This par 3 plays 144 yards, but at the tee, determine the Kentucky windage. Water and sand on the right, sand

and trees on the left. (Speaking of par 3s, on every course we played, we aimed for the center of the green, regardless of pin position. It served us well.)

The home hole is the most resistant to par on the back nine and is 420 yards. Driving to the 150-yard marker means a boom of 240 yards. It's nice to be out there because the approach has to take a well-bunkered green into account.

Between Cincinnati and Dayton is one of Jack Nicklaus's first efforts at design, the Grizzly, and one of his goals was to bring the PGA Tour to Warren County. He partnered with Desmond Muirhead for the job. Talk about reaching your goals. Not only did the PGA Tour show up to play, but so did the LPGA and the PGA Senior Tour. Especially the LPGA, which held a dozen major tournaments here.

But he had a second goal in mind, one that would seem contradictory. Nicklaus wanted trunk-slammers and ham-n-eggers to play and enjoy the course, as well. After all, it's not as if there is a wealth of daily-fee Nicklaus courses.

What does this mean to us? Well, it's sort of like, "Shake the hand that shook the hand," but in this case it's, "Oh, yeah, I played one of the Nicklaus courses … Matter of fact, it's one where he holds the course record, 62 … and where he won the first tournament." (Taking nothing from Nicklaus, but he also designed Muirfield for the Memorial and won it in 1977 and 1984.)

We think the place was a great opportunity for Nicklaus to learn that most esoteric of skills, designing golf courses. That same year, 1972, also began a sea change in golf balls; Spalding came out with the first two-piece ball. Suddenly, players were able to drive it farther into the woods.

The **Golf Center at Kings Island** (no, that's not a reference to Arnold Palmer) has two eighteen-hole courses, the Grizzly and the Bruin along with a four-hole warm up course called the Academy.

You're not going to believe this, but there was a time when the Bruin was lighted. At night. The Bruin is the mid-length course, under 3,500 yards, short par 3s and par 4s, and the longest is only 308 yards; par is 61, and there are no par 5s.

One more thing. The Academy Course. Now, this we haven't seen before. Doesn't mean it's unique, just that we haven't seen it before. The Academy is a four-hole warm-up/practice course. Two par 4s and two par 5s. Yardages are: 492 yards, 547 yards, 378 yards, and 377 yards and those are from the black tees. Tees are black, blue, white, and gold (forward).

His greens are as settled as they're going to get, and the Stimp is kept around 10, unless the big boys and big girls come to play.

This is right from the scorecard: " … Feel free to hit several shots from any location, but please do not hit more than five from any one location." Twenty bucks and you can stay all day long. Here's another difference between the Academy and the last executive course you played: conditioning and maintenance. So as it is on the Griz (as we like to say) and the Bruin, so it is throughout this golf complex. There is also a great pro shop here.

Ah, the conditioning. For starters, the grass is bent. The same superintendent has been tending his big, big garden for three decades. He wants to impress you and he will. His greens are as settled as they're going to get, and the Stimp is kept around 10, unless the big boys and big girls come to play. Then they are polished to resemble marble countertops.

On the Griz and Bruin, Nicklaus saved some trees to use as design elements, and then added his thoughts on sand bunkers and water. The terrain dips and rolls and most lies are level.

By selecting the proper tee, playing here is a joy. But don't get all full of yourself with a good score. Remember, the pro tours tee it up at the back of the box, the superintendent trims landing areas to make the path to success far more narrow, pin positions are often three paces from the edge of the green, and the surface of the green does its very good imitation of an asphalt parking lot.

Can you arrive early and warm up on the Academy? Then restrict yourself to three clubs and play the Bruin? And then, with a healthy sweat broken, attack the Grizzly? Darn right you can. And when your head hits the pillow that night, it's "Goodnight, Irene."

The pillows, like everything else at **Cincinnati Marriott Northeast**, are more comforting than a lullaby. Big, quiet, elegantly furnished rooms and suites. Suites are so nice we thought above upgrading the card game to chemin de fer. Not for long, of course. Close to the golf complex.

We liked the River City Grille. Two of us, city slickers from the get-go, had the Reuben sandwich. What better than a two-napkin sandwich so thick it strains your jaws? So good you don't add to the table conversation, busy as your jawbones are. Swiss cheese. Great rye bread. Thousand Island dressing. Extra dressing on the side. Corned beef. We think that sandwich covers all the major food groups except chocolate. We knew the chocolate cake was good, with or without ice cream, because the selfish, self-centered, egotistical galoot among us refused to share. Love the way another member handled the situation: "Be that way. You just saw your last gimme."

Today, nearly forty years later, the Grizzly owns the unique distinction of playing host to four tours: the PGA, LPGA, Senior Tour and the LPGA Duramed Futures. This is a testament to the fact that the Grizzly is one of the most versatile layouts in the state.

Many Nicklaus features adorn the course, including Jack's trademark multi-curved fairways, large trees retained as natural hazards, bunkers and water. With the aid of Desmond Muirhead, Nicklaus created a course in keeping with the times, a mere 6,500 yards from the tips.

"It was one of Jack's first designs and he knew this area would be a tourist destination for years to come," said Kings Island head pro Andy Horn, who began his twenty-third year at the facility in 2010. "The pros have played here for years but a lot of golfers can play this course."

Two spectacular par 5s are signature holes on the Grizzly. No. 9 on the North layout is just 490 yards but water is prominently in play as it is on No. 9 on the West layout, a more robust 550 yards and the number one handicap hole.

Among several challenges on the Grizzly are the five par 3 holes, three of which are over 200 yards. The par 4 third hole on the North nine is another tester—just 375 yards but a dogleg guarded on both sides by trees, trees and more trees.

The course is bent grass and the greens run a reasonable 10 on the Stimpmeter. Superintendent Dale Davenport has tended to the Kings Island facility for thirty years and "keeps the course in tournament shape year-round," according to Horn.

SHAKER RUN GOLF CLUB

4361 Greentree Rd.
Lebanon
513.727.0007
www.shakerrungolfclub.com

COURTYARD BY MARRIOTT HAMILTON

1 Riverfront Plaza
Hamilton
800.606.2813

WALDEN PONDS

6090 Golf Club Ln.
Indian Springs
513.785.2999
www.waldenponds.com

Hamilton, Ohio has something to offer. For a few generations, commercial paper plants and other industry kept Hamiltonians working steadily. Alas, the '80s were cruel to the town and industry packed up and left. Among other businesses crippled was the Hamiltonian Hotel, which suddenly found itself with no guests. There is no interstate highway close by, so the next guest was expected to be operating a wrecking ball.

Or as Oliver Hardy said to Stan Laurel, "Well, this is a fine kettle of fish."

Enter the Hamilton Community Foundation, one of those do-gooder groups with more energy and high hopes than opportunity. Their work is a very good example of, "If you don't ask, you don't get." They asked **Marriott** Corporation to buy the Hamiltonian Hotel. Long story short—Marriott bought it, and funneled $13 million into it. Thirteen millions dollars?

Yup, and as far as we're concerned, well worth it. Changes are myriad, every one of them for the better. Just a hint, but think about it: You, at the end the day, sitting on the back terrace, cigar in one hand, cold beer in the other, watching the Great Miami River dawdle along. The fire pit is blazing away. Nice way to put a cap on the day.

Inside, the improvements are dramatic. A big surprise to any guest who stayed at the old place and then walks into the new, as in, "where the heck am I?"

Full service restaurant, Amici's, and comfortable bar. Big things, such as renovated rooms that include our favorite, the king suite. Okay, here's another suggestion for getaway groups: Make sure The Guy gets the king suite and doesn't have to pay extra for it. The benefits? Two of them. First, it shows The Guy how much you appreciate all his organizational skills and second, it's a great room to play cards. Amenities include microwave and refrigerator.

Little things, such as newspaper and Starbucks coffee in the lobby if you're in a rush, bedding you can bounce a quarter off, and fresh, sweet air. We add that only because when industry blew town, they took the smell along with them and breathing in this farming area is sweet, indeed.

A stroll through this old and handsome town is highly recommended. Hamilton bills itself as the City of Sculpture, and no one is arguing. Sculpture throughout the town means an after-dinner walk turns into a leisurely affair.

Of course, our first secretary of the treasury, Alexander Hamilton, is there, and his statue is right next to Ryan's Tavern, named for the recent mayor, Don Ryan, who took an old building with sturdy bones and renovated it. It had been home to a newspaper and dress shop among other businesses and today pays homage to the Irish, including a menu with the traditional, seven-course, Irish dinner: six bottles of Guinness and a potato. Somewhat pricey at $200, and the staff knows if ever they sell one, the commission is one half. (How could you not fall in love with Hamilton?)

We said three things after dining at Amici's, the hotel restaurant: ravioli, ravioli, ravioli. We are realists and know that no ravioli is as good as an Italian mother-in-law's, but these little pasta pockets, jammed with a combination of cheeses, is darn near. You can give us all the salad and bread you want, but if good pasta is in front of us, those plates will go untouched. The menu also has the usual suspects such as beef, pork, and fish. When servers are taking plates to other tables, we also take a look at the plate. Some handsome presentations here.

Speaking of handsome presentations, **Shaker Run Golf Club** has long been known for its physical beauty, careful and meticulous maintenance, and, since we last played, another nine holes has been added. Think about it: 27 holes, nine by Michael Hurdzan and eighteen by Arthur Hills.

Out of respect, we brought out our Dress Golf outfit: an old and wonderful pair of Johnston & Murphy shoes (with a sole design not seen before or since) we bought fifteen or twenty years ago and wear only two or three times each season; cotton and linen pair of Alexander Julian slacks, and a Fairway & Green shirt fresh out of the plastic. If we would have thought about it, we would have visited our barber and manicurist, too.

If Hills's layout isn't the best in the area, well, then we've been hornswoggled. Hills didn't move much dirt when he created this course, and found surprises aplenty for players. His nines are named Woodlands and Lakeside; Hurdzan's nine is called the Meadows. To say players need every club in the bag is damning with faint praise; we could have used a couple extra.

The Woodlands, of course, uses stands of mature trees to define holes and guide players, and in this farm country, changes in elevation aren't expected. Allow us to disabuse you of that notion. The course is in Lebanon, just down the pike from the hotel, and suddenly there is elevation change enough to delight a bungee jumper. Stepping on to the fifth tee, a par 3 of a couple hundred yards, the green is hidden 'til you walk up to the edge of the cliff. The sheer cliff drops almost a hundred feet and that tiny green we see at the bottom is guarded by a pond and dangerous sand. Suddenly, golf skills heretofore not practiced come into play.

Okay, maybe it isn't all that dramatic, and yes, you can see where you're going, and no, it isn't off a cliff, and the 200-yard tee is from the tips, but still. The hole gives pause first for its perceived difficulty and then for its beauty. First-timers should be pleased with bogeys here. It gives pause because of the difficulty with club selection. Add to that the wind. Like your conscience, it is always there. Hitting the green is cause for high fives. (That reminds us of one of golf's great virtues: We enjoy seeing great shots as well as making them ourselves.)

The small greens designed by Hills are a challenge to the accuracy of any iron game; in addition, they have subtle breaks and Stimp at 11.

No. 9 is another memorable hole, a par 4 that perfectly uses Armco Lake. From a peninsula tee, to a peninsula green. Water comes into play three times on this nine, though it adds a visual treat on a half dozen. Flatlanders are advised bring out the camera. This hole has a fraternal twin in No. 9 on Lakeside, and mirrors its brother. On both, the question on the tee is, how much can you cut off? The difference between hope and reality is apparent just about the time you're picking up your tee.

Stop in the snack bar? This is not a typical snack bar. It has a name, The Shaker Bar and Grill. Bar filled with swing oil, of course, and a menu that titillates. Guys love being titillated. In addition to sandwiches and appetizers, the menu includes baby back ribs. It gets better. Or worse, depending on the last report from your cardiologist: hot fudge sundaes.

Wipe the drool from your chin; there are still nine holes to play. The Hurdzan nine was added a decade ago, an inspired addition that only makes Shaker an even better place to play.

His nine is markedly different, of course, and every bit as enjoyable. It is more open and the two par 3s are over water. Real men will play the ball they started with; the lesser among us reach in the bag for a shag ball.

Hurdzan might be the best at modern bunkering; they can serve as aiming points, hole definition, or landing areas for bad shots. Some are easy to leave, others beg you to hang around for another shot or two.

He didn't have the woods or water that Hills had, and after playing, we said, "Good thing he didn't or we'd still be out there." This nine is 3,560 yards, and big hitters are tempted. Go ahead.

As long as we were in the neighborhood of Ryan's Pub, we hung out an extra day to play nearby **Walden Ponds**, in Indian Springs, aptly named given the water on the course.

It can stretch to 7,000 yards, but only barely; from the tips it plays 7,001 yards, par 72. This track is another Hurdzan gem and you can see that as soon as you look at the huge greens and deep, high-lipped bunkers. Lots of flora and fauna, which is especially good, because housing is nearby. Not so close as to interfere, but they are there.

Both nines finish with par 5s. (A personal note: We think every course should begin and end with par 5s.) No one with us was able to reach in two, but they are reachable. Tall and ancient slabs of rock are here, quarried rock shore up moats. Hurdzan has been a master with rock; he makes holes more distinctive as well as good-looking with the stuff.

It was worth staying over; now, back to Ryan's Tavern.

MAY I PROPOSE A TOAST?

May I propose a toast? To the men and women who maintain our golf courses, the superintendents:

Every day they rise before daybreak for us, and at the end of the day, their clothes are stained with sweat, grass, and motor oil. They would have it no other way. (Hear, hear!)

They tolerate, though rarely indulge us. When we send a foot-long divot farther than the ball, then hold up the fairway's scalp, and say, "Is this a keeper?" Their curses are silent. (Hear, hear!)

Mother Nature calls them by their first names. (Hear, hear!)

They are chemists, arborists, landscapers, mechanics, goodwill ambassadors, friends of the earth, and an untapped market for manicurists. (Hear, hear!)

Often they are burned by Old Sol, drenched by the rains, hit by errant golf balls, and mistaken for Bigfoot. They suffer silently.

Old superintendents never die; their bodies are tossed on to the compost pile. (Hear, hear!)

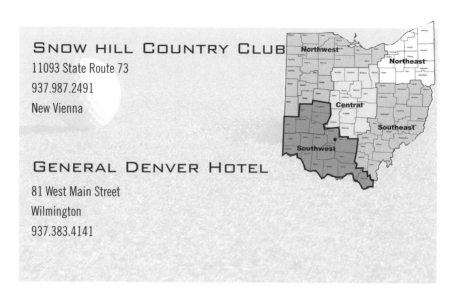

SNOW HILL COUNTRY CLUB

11093 State Route 73
937.987.2491
New Vienna

GENERAL DENVER HOTEL

81 West Main Street
Wilmington
937.383.4141

Once you park, you won't be back to the car until you leave. We like places like this. Fewer guys get lost. No need for a designated driver. More difficult to lose the car.

Snow Hill Country Club is quiet as a country churchyard, pretty as three ladies and a pair of jacks. Opened for play in 1924, this golf course is an octogenarian, but here, that's not considered old.

The clubhouse will soon be a bicentenarian. The big old frame is almost 200 years old, and once served as a stage coach stop. You're going to sit where the guy riding shotgun sat. Except he *really* sat shotgun. No surprise, there are ghosts here. If you don't believe us, ask head pro Doug Ledford. Ledford has a bit of history his own self with Snow Hill. He grew up playing this wonderful course, then blew town to earn his PGA card. Then he returned.

Anyway, according to legend, the place was also part of the Underground Railroad as well as a brothel. (Hmm. That would be two brothels in this book—the other is at Brennan's Fish House in Grand Harbor. Little wonder this is ... *the Guys' Guide.*) At both places, ghosts have unrestricted access. We tend to believe the legends here. After all, its original name was Buzzard's Glory.

At first glance at the scorecard, the course not intimidating. It plays a mere 6,500 yard from the tips. How tough could these old pushup greens be? Won't our new technology just make mincemeat out of the course? Snow Hill started life as a nine-hole course and in 1989 the other half was designed and built.

Take a second look. There are a couple clues on the scorecard that should give veteran golfers pause. Par is 70, but the slope is 129. Hmm. The course rating is 71.8. The first par 5 is more than 600 yards. The par 3s are long. Maybe we better play it a time or two before betting paper money.

Turns out there are more surprises on Snow Hill Country Club than we found on the Nixon Tapes. The fun begins with a par 5 that is reachable in two only for the divinely inspired. A dogleg left with trees hugging the left side. It's a three-shotter. And a formal introduction to the greens here. So a good opening hole. And No. 2 is a 186-yard par 3. Pushup greens? May be, but these babies undulate. (As we went on, we found the greens to be some of the best we played. Fast, true, challenging, and beautifully maintained. It was hard to find a ball mark that had not been repaired. Players here like and care for their course.) And next thing you know, we're on the third tee, looking down the 600-yard fairway, trying to see a flag.

We thought getting on in regulation was cause for high fives. There were no high fives. And the course didn't stop there; No. 4 is a 442-yard par 4 with a fairway split by water. It's the number one handicap hole. It was at this point we asked ourselves, "What have we gotten into?"

The course settled down a bit, lulling us, we discovered, before springing No. 8, a par 3 of 213 yards. At least it's downhill.

Stopped for a little swing oil at the turn and wished we could play the front nine again. Sure, it's a very challenging nine, but it's also a championship course in gorgeous condition. The rough here is just that—rough. Leaving the fairway, however briefly, puts a major impediment on the road to par.

More of the same, wonderful stuff on the back side. Great par 3s, and on No. 14, a peninsula green. No. 16 is a par 5 we loved the minute we saw the green, a plateau that might be worth a half club or more, depending on which way the wind is blowing. The green on the home hole is tough, but for a different reason—it's not deep and holding it calls for skill with the irons.

Back to the clubhouse. Snow Hill Country Club offers us benefits other places simply can't. We were talking with the manager, who told us a group of a dozen guys was coming in soon. For groups of eight or more, the professional chef will ignore the menu and plan dinners according to the group. The group coming in had steak and lobster waiting one night, cottage ham and green beans another.

There are five rooms upstairs and a staff member stays overnight to handle any emergencies. And to set up and service your poker game. Nice to have someone get the drinks, wipe down the table, show you where to go when you reach for the double corona. Maybe even sit in for you? The restaurant, except for groups, is open for breakfast and lunch only.

For dinner, the manager recommended **General Denver Hotel** in Wilmington, a nine-mile scoot. In an old and beautiful brick building, there are burgers, melts, chicken, BBQ beef, and turkey. Three steaks, too.

On draft is General Denver Pub Ale, worthy of a multi-stein sampling. Oh, yeah, drink fast. The General is an early closer: 9 p.m. on weekdays and 10 on Friday and Saturday.

When you tee it up the next day, you'll thank the General for tucking you in at a decent hour.

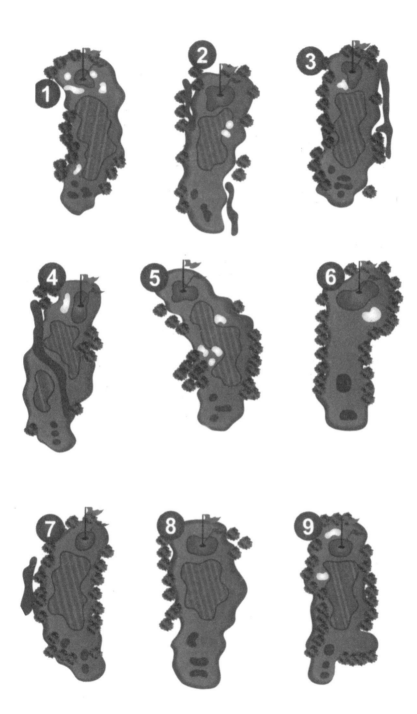

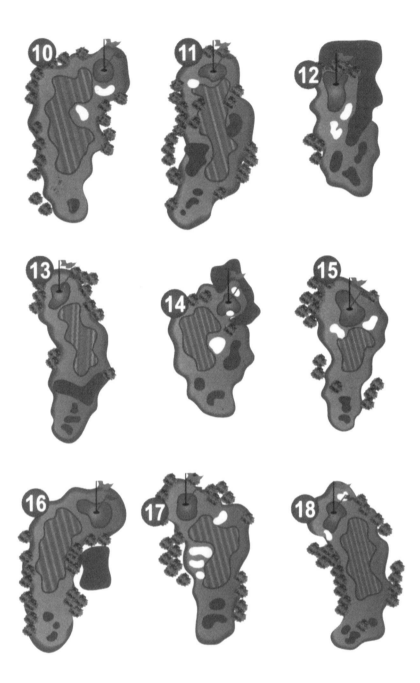

INDEX

LODGING

Northwest

Central

Northeast

Southeast

Southwest

Northwest
Bluto's Sports Bar and Grill, 23
Lemmy's Restaurant, 11
The Angry Bull, 14

Central
Max and Erma's, 67
Rusty Bucket, 61
The Place Off the Square, 33

Northeast
Arnie's West Branch Steak House, 124
Bravo Cucina Italiana, 135
Brennan's Fish House, 76
Carrabba's Italian Grill, 141
DeVore's Hopocan Gardens, 160
Ferrante Winery & Ristorante, 109
Handel's Homemade Ice Cream, 134

Southeast
Lighthouse Bistro, 177
Mrs. Yoder's Kitchen, 191

Southwest
Fleming's Prime Steakhouse, 219
Méla Urban Bistro, 208